Evergreen Pacific

Shellfish Guide

J. D. Wade

Evergreen Pacific
Publishing Ltd.
Shoreline, Washington

Photo & Illustration Credits

All photos and illustrations with the parenthetical (WDFW) were provided by the Washington State Department of Fish & Wildlife.

Cover Photo by Washington State Department of Fish & Widllife.

Photos on pages 41 & 76 by Barry Gregg.

All other photos were provided by the author.

Maps on pages 35-37 were provided by the author and Lee Wade.

All other illustrations were provided by Lee Wade.

To learn more about other Evergreen Pacific publications, visit our web site at: **www.evergreenpacific.com**

CONTENTS

ABOUT THE AUTHOR

J.D. Wade is a lifetime resident of the Puget Sound area in Washington state. He began playing and digging on shellfish beaches at an early age. As an adult he helped organize a Hood Canal seafood business, harvesting clams and oysters for private beach owners. He also was a commercial prawn fisherman.

J.D. has become a strong, vocal advocate of shellfish conservation and is well known by Washington state legislators, having testified many times on seafood conservation issues before the House and Senate Natural Resources Committees.

As a volunteer member of the Washington Department of Fish and Wildlife Crab Advisory Group, he keeps his finger on the pulse of Puget Sound shellfish issues.

J.D. has been a sought-after speaker at the Seattle Boat Show as well as many other sportsman's shows around the state. In this role, J.D. promotes the fun of shellfishing while at the same time he supports the conservation of our fragile resources.

INTRODUCTION

The northwest coast of North America is known for rugged natural beauty and abundant sea life. It's mild climate and clean ocean waters produce a home for a rich variety of marine life, including hundreds of species of shellfish.

Boaters and beachcombers thrive upon the tasty inhabitants of these waters and shores, taking great pride and enjoyment in gathering their own food from the environment.

Gathering shellfish is an outstanding family activity. Experiencing nature outdoors together is both bonding and rewarding, and the outcome will be a delicious meal. Even people who do not care for the flavor of fish, usually enjoy a good fresh shellfish dinner.

The anticipation of pulling up a crab trap is exciting. Digging in the sand in pursuit of a clam is therapeutic. Counting the number of shrimp in the trap that just came aboard can be rewarding or disappointing, but never boring. Kids love the activities.

This book is intended to present to the recreational shellfish gatherer an overview of the most popular types of edible shellfish, what type of areas to locate them in, and how to harvest, cook and eat them. Included in this book are suggested recipes for preparing your catch while still on the beach, back at your campsite, aboard your boat, or at home.

The Shellfish Guide will explore not only gathering, but storing, cooking and eating your culinary rewards. The reader will learn the best ways to do it all. Hopefully shellfish gathering will become a family adventure that will lead to many years of togetherness and healthy meals.

Plan the outing by studying charts together and making a list of necessary tools and baits required. Don't forget safety and comfort items. Life vests, warm clothes and snacks are as important as the tools needed for a fun family outing. A wet, cold, and hungry experience might leave a lasting negative impression, but proper preparation will yield an enjoyable experience which everyone will want to repeat.

Enjoy, and bon appétit.

CLAMS

There are many species of clams along North America's west coast, but only a handful are of interest to recreational boaters and sportsmen. They are found on the open coast and inland bays and harbors. Although clams can be found in nearly all areas, it's getting increasingly harder to distinguish public beaches from private. Much care must be exercised in determining where it is legal and proper to dig for these delicious nuggets. Usually government-owned tidelands are open for harvest. (See charts included in this chapter and the appendixes.)

Clams are subterranean water filters. They live under the beaches drawing water through their siphon-like necks, filtering out food particles, primarily plankton. The water is then discharged back toward the surface. In sandy or muddy beaches this discharge creates water geysers at low tides, or holes, which give away the clam's location. Clams are also called "intertidal" shellfish, in that they live in that area between the lowest tide and the highest tide on a beach.

This filtering action creates the next concern. Clams filter out and retain pollutants from the water, so one must consider the environmental conditions before harvesting and eating clams.

In this chapter we will look at clam species in order of desirability: Razor Clams, Littleneck Clams, known as "steamers," Butter Clams, Geoduck, and Horse Clams.

RAZOR CLAMS:

This variety of beach dwellers has a sweet, succulent flavor, causing it to be widely considered the world's best tasting clam. Razor clams can be found on sandy beaches of coastline from northern California to Alaska's Aleutian Islands. They are always found below Mean Low Low Water, which means you can only harvest them during "minus" low tides. They will usually be found near the sand's surface, but that does not mean they are easy to catch. Yes, I said "catch." They can move FAST!

Siliqua Patula, alias Razor Clam, have thin elongated shells covered with a shiny, tan periostracum (skin).

Siliqua Patula, as they are known in science books, reach maturity in just two years, growing to an average of four and a half inches in length and two inches in width. These tasty delicacies are prized by the public, and are hardly ever found in seafood stores. Therefore, thousands of people gather on beaches during open season low tides. In order to protect the clam population, seasons are very restricted. In Washington state there is no commercial harvest allowed except by tribes. In Oregon and B.C. very limited commercial harvest is allowed by nontribal individuals.

Refer to the local game regulations for seasons and bag limits. Whatever the limit, diggers must keep the first number of clams to meet the state limits. Small clams can't be discarded in order to fill a limit with bigger clams.

Since razor clams taste so good and the season is so restricted, let's look at how you can make the best use of your time to catch your limit.

A 15 clam Washington State limit of Razor Clams. Note the shellfish license which is required to be worn visibly when digging clams or crab fishing. (WDFW)

People crowd the beaches for a single day at a time of Razor Clam harvest. (WDFW)

Suppose a season opening has been announced and you've driven your family to the beach, equipped with all the proper shellfish licenses and equipment. Each person needs his/her own container for holding a separate clam limit. The digging implement can be shared, but remember, you will only have a short time to dig. No more than two persons should share one tool between them.

The best digging time will be an hour before to an hour after the low tide. If the tide is before daylight, good lights are a must. Headlamps combined with lanterns are handy. Flashlights are clumsy as you need both hands free for digging, and since you are at the water's edge, anything you lay on the sand is vulnerable to incoming waves. Yes, sometimes you can get wet when on your knees and about to catch up with a fleeing clam, and the

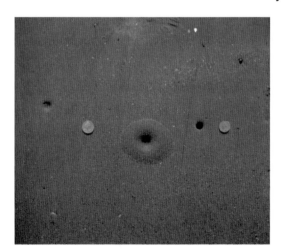

Clam vent holes are called a "show." Usually the larger show means a larger clam. The center show with a "halo" means the clam is close to the surface. Note the dimes for size comparison. (WDFW)

unnoticed wave approaches. It's all part of the fun. A change of shoes, socks and pants is handy to have on hand.

You will be looking for the "show." No, it's not movie time. The show here is a depression in the sand or a hole. The larger the show the larger the clam that made it. These shows are made when the tip of the clams neck, which is close to the surface, is retracted, causing the depression, or when it "vents" itself when feeding, creating the hole. You can make the clam show itself by stomping around in ten-foot diameter circles, then watching for a show. Kids love doing this, but they may not be heavy enough to make the show. However, it does burn off energy, which is always good to do at the beach.

A "clam gun" is a very specialized shovel tool, designed just for digging razor clams. Its long narrow blade is angled just right for chasing fast-moving clams, and it has a short, stout handle. Most good clam diggers will open a hole in the sand on the water side of the show, then drop to their knees,

How to Dig With a Clam Shovel

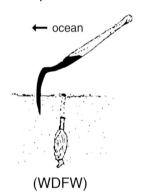

← ocean

1. Place the shovel blade 4 to 6 inches seaward of the clam show. The handle of the shovel should be pointed toward the sand dunes.

(WDFW)

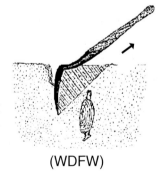

2. Use your body weight to push the shovel blade straight into the sand while you drop to one knee. In hard sand, gently rock the shovel handle from side to side for ease of entry. It is very important to keep the blade as vertical as possible to keep from breaking the clam shell.

(WDFW)

3. Pull the handle back just enough to break the suction in the sand, still keeping the blade as straight as possible. The sand will crack as shown.

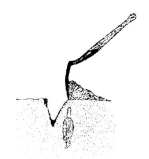

(WDFW)

4. Succeeding scoops of sand expose the clam enough to reach down with your hand and grasp its shell. Razor clams move rapidly downward but not horizontally. Make sure you keep the first 15 clams and avoid wasting any.

(WDFW)

and dig like a dog burying a bone, as fast as possible. This way the elusive clam can be felt and retrieved without breaking its shell.

Newer modern technology brought about the invention of the "clam tube." This is a hollow, metal, two-foot-long tube, four inches in diameter. It's open on one end, closed on the other, with a half inch air vent hole and handles. Facing the ocean, you should center the clam tube over the show, slant the top of the tube slightly toward yourself and push down with a rocking or twisting motion, leaving the air vent uncovered. This will keep you in line with the clam's descent. Work the tube down 6" to 10", then cover the air vent and pull up. Use your leg muscles, keeping the back straight

Clam Tube with 15-clam limit (WDFW)

to avoid muscle strain. Release the air vent, emptying the tube, then go back down the hole another six or eight inches after the clam. The suction created by pulling the sand out of the hole can be quite heavy. Take your time with this method. The clam will not out-dig you. It is easier to remove two or more sand cores from the tube before catching the clam. Check each core that you bring up. The clam may be concealed within.

Even though this method was designed to make razor clam digging easier, there are definite drawbacks. The tube is only four inches wide, allowing less then an inch of clearance on either side of mature clams, leading to many broken shells. Back muscle strain is common and even heart attacks can be brought on from the effort of lifting. Be cautious and take your time. Rest a lot between "battles."

Since their shells can be easily broken by contact with digging implements or rough handling during the battle, most agencies require you to keep every razor clam dug, regardless of size or condition. For safety's sake, the states request you fill your holes.

Tip: For the safety of humans and beach dwellers, always fill in your holes when digging for any species of clam. The fresh pile of material removed from your excavation may plug the airway of whatever creature is living beneath the beach surface, leading to

Kids love digging clams. (WDFW)

6

death. Some clam-digging tides occur at night, and open holes in the darkness are obvious human safety hazards. If the incoming tide covers a hole, someone can take a nasty, wet tumble.

Once you've caught your limit, it is time to clean them. All razor clams should be cleaned before cooking. The meat can be removed from the shell by simply submerging the clams in boiling water for a few seconds, or pouring boiling water over them. When the shell pops open, put the clams immediately into cold water and remove the meat. Another way is to cut the four attachments of the paired adductor muscles by running a knife blade along the inner surface of each shell. There are several ways to clean razor clams, but the basic aim is to remove the gills and digestive tract, the dark parts of the clam. The following commercial procedure for "steaking" clams for frying is done with a sharp knife or scissors.

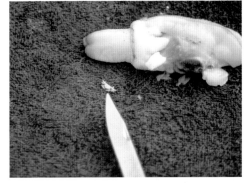

"Pea Crab" are found under the shells of some species of large clams. They pose no health threat to either the host clam or humans. Simply discard them.

Then snip off the tip of the neck.

Cut open the body from the base of the neck.

The gills and foot are separated with two cuts.

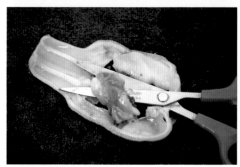

A circular cut of the foot will remove the gut. After removing the gut, slit the foot so it lies flat.

Rinse, and the steak is ready for further preparation.

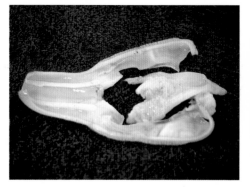

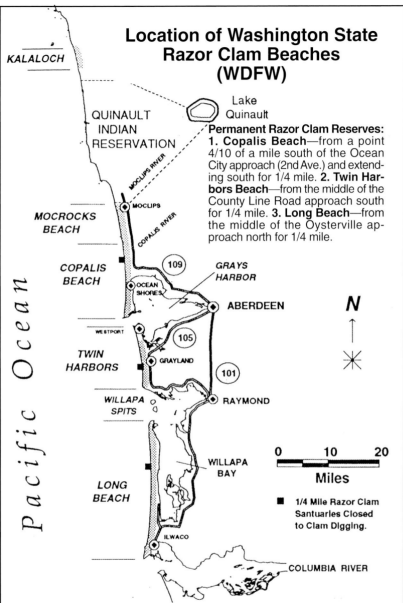

Location of Washington State Razor Clam Beaches (WDFW)

KALALOCH

QUINAULT INDIAN RESERVATION

Lake Quinault

MOCLIPS RIVER

MOCLIPS

MOCROCKS BEACH

COPALIS RIVER

COPALIS BEACH

109

OCEAN SHORES

GRAYS HARBOR

ABERDEEN

WESTPORT

105

TWIN HARBORS

GRAYLAND

101

WILLAPA SPITS

RAYMOND

LONG BEACH

WILLAPA BAY

ILWACO

COLUMBIA RIVER

Pacific Ocean

Permanent Razor Clam Reserves:
1. Copalis Beach—from a point 4/10 of a mile south of the Ocean City approach (2nd Ave.) and extending south for 1/4 mile. **2. Twin Harbors Beach**—from the middle of the County Line Road approach south for 1/4 mile. **3. Long Beach**—from the middle of the Oysterville approach north for 1/4 mile.

N

0   10   20
Miles

■ 1/4 Mile Razor Clam Santuaries Closed to Clam Digging.

Razor clam sanctuaries (Reserves) are 1/4 mile sections of coastal ocean beaches located on three beach areas that are used to assist in the management of the razor clam resource. The three areas are marked with large metal or wooden posts and are adequately signed to designate a no-digging area. Sampling occurs on a continuing basis for various population studies and comparisons with harvested areas.

LITTLENECK CLAMS ("STEAMERS"):

There are two types of little neck clams on the west coast: the native one, and a hybrid import from Japan known as "Manila." All these succulent little nuggets are easy to find, easy to harvest, and wonderful table fare.

Littleneck clams can be found on the coastline from lower California to Alaska. They are main dinner courses for thousands of boaters and beach combing campers each year. Native littlenecks are small, seldom more then two inches wide, and vary in color from white to grey to light brown. They are indigenous to the northwest and can be found on gravel beaches, usually ones which contain some small to pea size stones, where the larvae can safely attach during spawn cycles. They are very prolific. When the spawns occur, the larvae can spread up to fifty miles, drifting along with the currents. This is how the imported Japanese Manila variety has spread throughout the Northwest. Lying alongside the natives in many of the same beds, the manilas are a different color. Dark purple to black, with white or yellowish marbling, they are also more oblong in shape. Normally they will be found between mid tide to low tide ranges. These clams will seldom be found more than six inches below the beach surface, and, unlike other clam species, will rarely be found on sandy beaches.

Top Left: Eastern Soft-shell Clam (pointed)
Top Right: Butter Clam
Center: Cockle
Lower Left: Manilla Clam
Lower Right: Native Littleneck Clam

(WDFW)

Manila littleneck clam
Tapes philippinarum
Average size is 1-2", up to 2 1/2". Oblong shell has concentric and radiating lines. May have colored, patterned shells. Found to 4" below surface.

Cockle clam
Clinocardium nuttali
Prominent, evenly-spaced ridges which fan out from the hinge. Mottled, light brown. Can grow to 5". Found just below surface.

Native littleneck clam
Protothaca staminea
Average size is 1-2", up to 2-1/2". Rounded shell has concentric and radiating lines. Found 6-10" below surface.

Butter clam
Saxidomus giganteus
Average size is 3-4", up to 6". Shells are usually chalky-white with no radiating ridges. The siphon can be pulled into its shell. Usually found 12-18" below the surface.

As of the date of this edition, the above 4 species have a 1 1/2" min. size limit.

(Not to scale)

Geoduck clam
Panopea abrupta
Heavy, oblong shell, rounded at one end. Appears cut-off at the other. The siphon can't be retracted. Found 2-3 feet below surface. Can weigh up to 10 lbs.

Horse clam
Tresus capax (shown)
Tresus nuttalli (not shown)
Large, can be up to 8". Shell is chalky-white with yellow-brown patches of "skin." The siphon can't be pulled into shell and has a leather-like flap on the tip. Found 1-2 feet below surface.

(Eastern) Softshell clam
Mya arenaria
Can grow to 6". Shells are soft, chalky-white with a rough, irregular surface. Shell is rounded at the foot end, pointed at the siphon end. Found to 18" below surface.

(WDFW—illustrations provided to WDFW by Roby Bowman, Debbie Bacon, and Darrell Pruett)

11

TIP: Littlenecks can be found under beach boulders. Roll the stone aside and check the bottom of the remaining depression.

TIP: Most of the time, you will find littleneck clams under any oyster beds you encounter.

TIP: Clams must be kept alive until time to cook. Keep them cool and damp. If possible, keep them in a bag suspended in salt water. This will also "purge" them, allowing them to naturally flush out sand. A better way to purge them is to place them in a bucket of salt water and throw in a handful of corn meal. They will take in the meal, expelling their grit. The shell normally will be closed, as long as they are alive, or will quickly close when touched. Discard any that do not close before cooking. After cooking the shell should be open. Discard any still closed after cooking because that is also an indication that the clam was dead before cooking.

BUTTER CLAMS:

These are the big and husky specimens of the sweet clam family. They have thick shells growing to five-inch diameters, and hang out deeper underground. They have an excellent flavor, making them worth the extra digging effort required to harvest them.

Butter clams can be found near the low water mark on a variety of beach surfaces. You will find them in sand, pea gravel, or even between large rocks on a gravel beach. If the tide is not low enough, you will need to look in the water, as they can be found in water up to depths of 60 feet.

Small butter clams are often mistaken for littlenecks because they can be found near the surface along with littlenecks, and taste nearly as good. Their color will vary, depending upon the surrounding sand or gravel colors. Primarily greyish-white, they can be yellow, brown, or even black.

Just as other clam populations seem to be in colonies, butters will be found in clumps. Where there is one, more will be nearby, with the larger ones lying deeper, under the smaller.

COCKLE CLAMS:

The cockle clam is so similar to littleneck clams and the butter clam that it is hard to distinguish among them, especially when wet and covered with sand or mud. Only with two different kinds of these clams side by side can you tell the cockle clam by its more pronounced ridges. It can be found in the same habitat and cooked in the same manner as steamers and butter clams.

TIP: Littleneck clams, butter clams, and cockle clams, unlike razor clams, have a size limit. (Consult your state shellfish regulations.) If the clam is under the limit size, place the clam back in the hole in which you found it.

HORSE CLAMS:

The common view of these abundant, thin-shelled, deep-digging bivalves is that they are large, tasteless, and tough. Most folks think the only good use for a horse clam is as crab or bottomfish bait. Actually, they are quite flavorful when used in chowder.

Horse Clams (WDFW)

Adult horse clams can reach 8 inches in diameter, and are found one to two feet deep on sandy beaches, in the lowest third of tidal zones. Because their siphons (necks) are so long, they can squirt fountains of water into the air at low tide, and still be so deep it will take an excavation to dig them out. They range from California to Alaska.

Their shells are white, with a thin brownish covering that easily flakes off when exposed to the air. Because their necks are so long, horse clams frequently are mistaken for geoducks. They can be distinguished by the tip of the neck being leathery and usually covered with barnacles, whereas the geoduck has smooth skin over its entire neck.

13

TIP: Pea crabs are typically found under the shells of large species of clams. They are tiny little white crawlies, with soft shells of less then an inch in diameter, and completely harmless to humans or their host clams. Simply discard them.

GEODUCK CLAMS:

Pronounced "gooey-duck," these huge, ugly clam monsters are tastier than they appear. They are only found during the very lowest tides of the year, in sandy or muddy beaches, dug in at 18 inch to four foot depths. Their average weight is a meal-size 2-1/2 pounds, with larger specimens being common. They are such a popular clam that areas regularly accessible to diggers are wiped out, and only during the lowest minus tides (minus 2 feet or better) are the untouched beds accessible. Extreme minus tides like these occur perhaps 20 times a year, further restricting the sport harvest.

Geoduck (WDFW)

Geoducks can be found by the appearance of their siphon sticking out of the ground, but they are most easily seen while still underwater. They can be harvested quite efficiently by divers, or you may locate some while snorkeling. When you discover one, another will be nearby. Bed densities can be as high as one per square foot. They prefer areas with a soft sand and mud bottom, which further limits accessibility. They cannot tolerate the higher salinity of the ocean, and therefore are found only in bays and canals but not along the coast. A five-year-old geoduck shell measures five and a half inches, but the siphon (neck) often extends up to 36 inches.

DIGGING GEODUCKS: Do you know where you can borrow a steam shovel? The huge reward you will gain when you finally get one of these giant clams out of the ground will be worth the effort, but it will be effort. Hard work and muddy clothes will be part of the price you pay.

Kids have a ball doing this type of thing. Don your best Tom Sawyer face and provide them with a shovel with a long sturdy handle. You can tell them the popular story that the geoduck is trying to flee and is digging down as fast as it can. Actually, it doesn't move much, but as it retracts its siphon-like neck, it gives the impression of trying to out-dig the sand-flinging shoveler with clam chowder on his mind.

Most folks dig a trench alongside the clam, deep enough to get below the shell, then cave the trench in, searching for the dinner entree. Don't pull on the neck; you'll pull it off, and it's illegal to possess only a geoduck neck. Just keep probing and digging until you free the whole object. Rinse it off and store it in a wet gunny sack. Daily limit in most areas is three.

CLEANING: The neck can be cut up or ground up in chowder, after rinsing out sand and grit. The body meat, sliced open and entrails removed, can be pounded flat and sautéed, resembling abalone.

(EASTERN) SOFTSHELL CLAMS:

The softshell clam got its name because of its chalky-white, fragile shell. The shell is rounded at the foot end and tapered at the siphon end. Because of its chalky-white shell and because its siphon cannot be completely withdrawn, softshell clams are often mistaken for small horse clams. Softshell clams average four to six inches in length and are found on muddy or sandy beaches, often near the mouths of rivers. They are buried in a depth of eight to eighteen inches. Like the horse clam, they are known more for their use as crab or bottomfish bait than as an edible delicacy.

WHERE THE CLAMS ARE

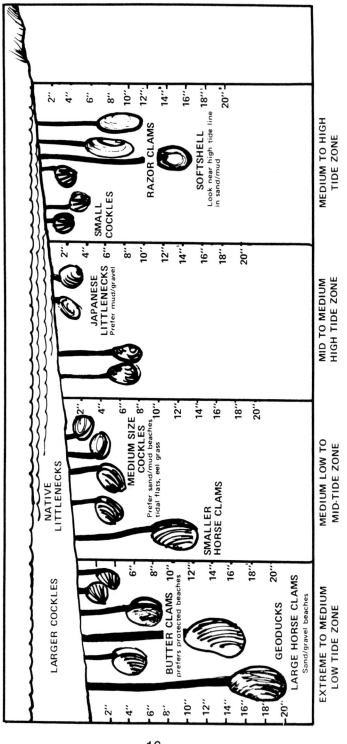

LARGER COCKLES

NATIVE LITTLENECKS

JAPANESE LITTLENECKS
Prefer mud/gravel

SMALL COCKLES

RAZOR CLAMS

SOFTSHELL
Look near high tide line in sand/mud

MEDIUM SIZE COCKLES
Prefer sand/mud beaches tidal flats, eel grass

SMALLER HORSE CLAMS

BUTTER CLAMS
prefers protected beaches

GEODUCKS

LARGE HORSE CLAMS
Sand/gravel beaches

EXTREME TO MEDIUM LOW TIDE ZONE

MEDIUM LOW TO MID-TIDE ZONE

MID TO MEDIUM HIGH TIDE ZONE

MEDIUM TO HIGH TIDE ZONE

16

CRABS

How can something as mean looking as a crab taste so good? One of the most popular family outdoor activities is crab fishing. Kids of all ages love doing it, and the end result is usually a crab eating festivity.

Kids love crabbing, making the sport a great family acitivity.

The North American west coast has abundant numbers of Dungeness and Red Rock Crab creating a multimillion dollar commercial harvest industry and a huge sportfishing industry. Crab are very important to the economy and they are really fun to catch. Let's take a look at how and where to find these tasty crustaceans.

Any body of salt water which has a mud or sandy bottom will probably contain crab. They can also be found along the edges of river mouths. To prevent being swept away, crab need the loose bottom material to burrow into during strong tidal changes. Crab are particularly fond of eel grass. It provides cover for them to hide, and for sneaking up on food.

When tides are changing rapidly, creating strong currents, crab become dormant, buried below the bottom surface or backed up against a piling or other bottom structure. As the currents ease, they come out of hiding with their appetites raging. That's why the best crabbing times are an hour before or an hour after a slack tide, high slack being best. (Slack tide is that time when the tide is at its lowest or highest point, and the tide is neither going in or out.)

Dungeness Crab are the favorite species. The meat is flavorful and they can grow up to ten inches across. Because crab are enclosed in a rigid exterior skeleton, they can grow only by shedding their shells. They molt up to seven times during the first year and at a decelerating rate in subsequent years, but each is on its own cycle. Some can be soft in a particular harbor at any time of the year. A size of four inches is reached in two years, and five and three-quarter inches in three years. Male crab mature a year or more before reaching the minimum legal size for harvesting, and females are completely protected from legal harvest. With large females producing up to two and a half million eggs each winter, there is no fear of overharvesting the resource under present regulations.

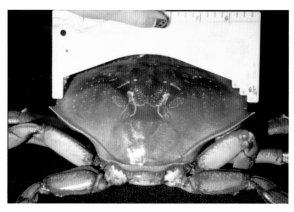

Minimum size requirements are measured across the back shell inside the outer points.

Dungeness Crabs have a purple-tinged, orange-brown shell with white-tipped claws and usually reach six to seven inches across the back. They are mainly found north of Tacoma, throughout Hood Canal, and along the coast. They range from the low intertidal down to 750 feet.

Dungeness Crab move about in "migration clusters," usually moving from deep water to shallow during the first six months of the year. The coastal specimens have a tendency to travel north. When they travel, the females remain separate from the males. If you are catching only females, it usually helps to move a hundred yards and see whether you

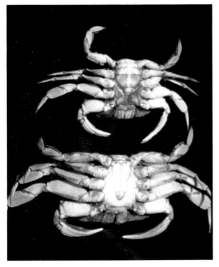
The female abdomen flap (top crab) is wide compared to the narrow male abdomen flap (bottom crab).

begin catching all males. Some crab really pack their bags and move out. One, tagged and released off Westport, Washington, was captured more then eighty miles south, at Tillamook Bay, Oregon. Oregon tagged crabs have traveled from Tillamook Bay northward to Willapa Bay, Washington.

With a keen sense of smell and poor eyesight, these eight-legged creatures prefer to sit and wait for food to come to them. That's why divers will find them protecting their "territory" at the base of rocks or pilings. The biggest specimens will have hollowed out impressions and become very aggressive if anything comes too near. That's why I instruct people to lower a trap directly next to a dock, rather then throwing it

---

WHY ARE ALL THE CRAB DYING?
During summer months, state fisheries' departments will routinely receive calls that huge numbers of crab have died. When crab shed their shells during molting, they completely back out of the old skeleton, leaving the impression that the remains are a dead crab. So the answer is, they are not dying but simply putting on a new spring-summer wardrobe, in what has to be one of nature's most interesting phenomena.

out as far as they can, as so many do.

When they move, they can be very quick, moving sideways in a true "crab-like" motion. I dropped a food morsel into a lagoon one day, and watched a sculpin (bullhead fish) and a crab race for it. They were both about 30 feet away in different directions. The crab got the food first! Let's look at the food they like best:

BAITS: The main thing to remember is that crab like "fresh" food. There's an "old wives tale" that crab like rotten bait. WRONG! Their favorite culinary delights are, in this order: clam meat, filleted fish carcasses (not just heads) chicken, turkey and beef. But all must be fresh! Your "freezer-burned" offerings will be accepted, but if you put a "freezer-burned" piece of fish in a trap next to a trap baited with the same type of fresh fish, you will see better results with the fresh item.

I researched this extensively when I was developing a new crab bait for retail sale. I tried fish, chicken and turkey alone, and combined with various other substances. The absolutely best concoction consisted of equal amounts of fresh ground salmon carcass, after filleting (bottom fish works as well), mixed with fresh ground chicken necks and backs.

CRABBING THE OREGON COAST

Along the Oregon coast, nearly all crabbing is done from jetties at the mouths of rivers. Unfortunately, there is a large number of seals and sea lions along the coast. Since the preferred type of trap is a ring, which stays put in the river currents better then a pot, the sea mammals can get directly to the bait used, competing with the crab for it.

Enter the Idaho mink rancher. This mink rancher had a problem disposing of his mink carcasses each year, until he discovered crab like this flavor while sea mammals are repelled by it. So each spring he packs up all his frozen mink carcasses, loads them in a refrigerated 18 wheeler, and sells them up and down the Oregon coast. Buy and use them while they last.

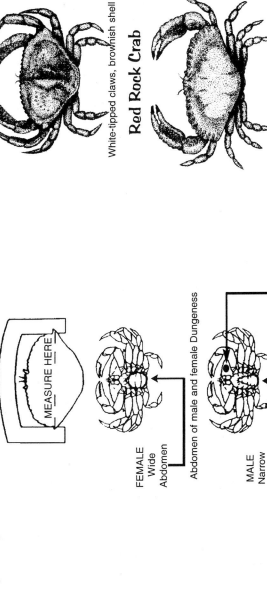

Where and How to Measure for Minimum Size

Caliper measurement at the widest part of the shell just in front of rear most point or tips.

MEASURE HERE

FEMALE Wide Abdomen

Abdomen of male and female Dungeness

MALE Narrow Abdomen

Check for soft shell here

Dungeness Crab

White-tipped claws, brownish shell

Red Rock Crab

Black-tipped claws, reddish shell, shell much wider than long

(WDFW)

The Life Cycle of a Crab
From Egg to Adult

Note that baby crabs look more like baby shrimp. Baby crabs look so different from adults that scientists once thought they were a different animal.

The female has been holding her fertilized eggs for months. She flaps her abdomen to release larvae hatching from 1 to 2 million eggs, each egg about the size of a grain of salt.

As the larvae shed the egg membrane, their spines harden to discourage predators from eating them. Salmon in net pens sometimes get these spiny larvae in their gills, contributing to fish kills.

In a brief prelarval stage, the prezoea drift out from the shore eating plankton.

The crab begins to develop its 10 legs as it drifts back into shallow water. Its mavillipeds help it swim, something adult Dungeness crabs don't do well.

The juvenile crab is essentially a shrimp with a small abdomen folded tightly beneath its body. From now on the crab will molt its shell several times as it grows. Each growth step is called an instar.

The larvae develop into a shrimp-like creature called a megalops. At this stage the crab is about the size of a large mosquito. Schools of megalops seek out appropriate habitat close to shore.

This I did with a commercial meat grinder, dropping equal portions into the vat. The fish provided the flavor of preference, and the chicken carried the flavor into the currents with an oily, long lasting texture.

HOW AND WHERE? A completely enclosed crab trap is called a "pot," and traps that lie completely flat on the bottom are called "ring traps" or "star traps." Pots are commonly used only part of each year, but ring-traps, star-traps or collecting by hand is normally legal yearlong in all areas. When a state department of fisheries determines a significant "molt" is occurring in an area, they will close the area to the use of pots. Crab have very soft shells when molting, and if they are caught in enclosed traps in this condition they can easily

Pots, when & where they are legal, can be left unattended, but ring-traps should be pulled up every 10 to 15 minutes.

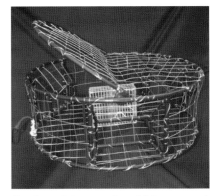

Crab pot-traps should be round with large doors allowing easy entry for the crab.

damage each other and be damaged by human hands trying to empty the traps. Soft shelled crab can escape one another's claws when in an open ring, and can easily be released unharmed when brought to the surface in one.

The best pots are round ones. Because square crab pots have corners, a sideways walking crab encountering a corner will likely just keep on moving away from the trap, never finding the door. If you use a round trap, the sideways traveler will keep going around the trap until it finds the door. All pots must be equipped with a means for escape if the pot is lost. Otherwise it could continue to "fish" for a long time, killing everything that gets trapped. There must be

Hoop Trap for Dock (Crabbing)

The preferred rig for dock crabbing has 2 hoops with collapsible mesh netting between them. Tie line on edge of dock and drop baited trap over the side. Trap will lay flat on bottom. Jerk up quickly every 10-15 minutes. Remember to tie bait securely to center of bottom mesh panel.

Basket-Type Crab Trap

All buoys must have (one) name, address and date clearly written upon them. Buoys must be constructed of durable material (no bleach, antifreeze, no detergent bottles, paint cans, etc.). Buoys must be visible on the surface at all times except during extreme tidal conditions. To indicate a crab trap, the buoy should be half red and half white, with both colors visible when in a floating position.

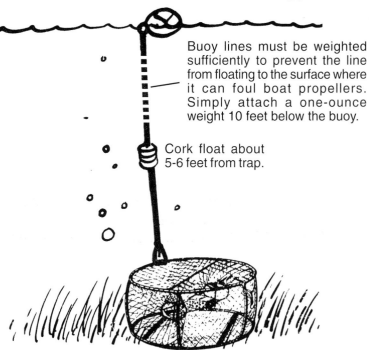

Buoy lines must be weighted sufficiently to prevent the line from floating to the surface where it can foul boat propellers. Simply attach a one-ounce weight 10 feet below the buoy.

Cork float about 5-6 feet from trap.

an escape opening protected by untreated cotton cord, and the access lid must be secured with the same cotton cord. If the pot is lost, in a few days the cord will rot away and anything inside can get out.

Your choice of fresh bait should be secured in the center of your selected trap either in a bait box, or, as I prefer, in a bait bag. A bag holds larger odd shaped pieces of bait, and allows the crustaceans a more direct access to their food. This will hold their attention better, giving the fisherman bet-

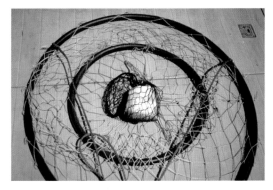

Ring-traps are legal for use all year in all areas. Secure bait in center of small ring.

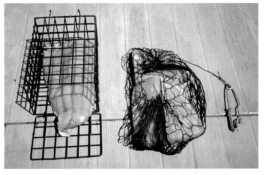

Bait "boxes" are fine, but bait "bags" work better. Bait must be fresh.

ter odds of catching them, especially in a ring or star trap. A crab's claws are made for crunching, not cutting, so they cannot cut through a mesh bag.

When fishing from a dock or jetty, no identification is required for the trap, but a shellfish license worn in a visible place is required for the fisherman. When deploying traps from a boat, a red and white float must be attached to your line. Each buoy must have the angler's name and address. There must be a one-ounce weight attached to the line ten feet below the buoy to prevent entangling the line in boat propellers. Be sure to use enough line to reach bottom with enough left over to allow for incoming tide and currents. Most recreational crabbing is done in sixty feet of water or less, but commercial pots can be found in waters as deep as 150 feet.

Pots can be left unattended for long periods, but rings must be "worked." Lower your ring straight down, making sure the bait stays in the center. Pull quickly every 10 to 15 minutes. Remove your legal keepers but leave a couple small ones in your ring or pot, and gently lower back to the bottom. The little ones will go right back to eating. They won't eat your bait very fast, but will make a clacking sound that will draw additional large crabs. Some folks will even secure a small strobe light with the bait, to further attract dinner. Crab respond to smell, light, and sound.

Each state's coastline, bays and sounds have public docks, piers, and jetties where crab can be caught. Many are handicapped accessible. Most ferry landings have a public fishing area, but remember to stay off railroad trestles. They are illegal and dangerous places to be caught.

YOUR CATCH: Be familiar with the local catch regulations before beginning your outing. Different areas around each state have different size and bag limits per species, plus set fishing times and dates. Legal sizes for male Dungeness vary from five and three-quarters inches in Oregon, to six and one quarter inches in Washington, and 165 mm (six and one half inches) in British Columbia. Either sex of Red Rock Crab can be collected in most areas, but only male Dungeness may be kept. Soft-shell, or molting crab, can be identi-fied by pressing the

Check for soft-shell "molting" condition by squeezing the leg sections. They should be firm rather than soft as this one is.

largest section of any leg. The section should be firm and will be full of meat. When molting, there will be little meat, not much flavor, and it will cost you a substantial fine if you're caught with one.

Red rock crabs have heavy, brick-red shells and black-tipped claws. They are smaller than Dungeness crab, ranging in size from five to seven inches. They are found throughout Puget Sound and prefer rocky bottoms with little silt, often hidden under rocks or partly buried under gravel or mud. They range from the mid-intertidal down to 260 feet.

After you have determined the proper sex and species of your catch, and it's large enough and firm, you may retain it in an empty container. Do NOT fill it with water. The inhabitants will quickly exhaust the oxygen in the water and actually drown. They simply need to be kept cool and damp. Cover them with a damp gunnysack. If you are going to be holding them for more then a couple hours you can occasionally cover them with seawater to revive them, but don't let them stay covered more then a few minutes. Never put them on, or covered with ice. They may freeze or drink the melting fresh water and die.

Crab should always be cooked alive (more on that later) to prevent toxins from deceased organs contaminating the meat. They can be kept alive overnight by wrapping them in wet material or newspapers, and placing them in the refrigerator. Do not allow the material to dry out. They will become dormant overnight, and you can tell if they are still alive in the morning by tweaking a "feeler" and watching for eye movement. They can be temporarily revitalized by immersing in cold water.

COOKING: The best means of cooking crab is to clean them first. Some folks feel it is more "humane" that way, but the most important reason is to prevent contaminating the meat with any undesirable elements remaining on the shell or in the inedible internal organs. Most specimens will be caught with bottom muck and slime covering them, stuff we don't want to cook into our succulent meat. It is also much less messy, less smelly, and you can get much more into your cooking pot. See the following photo series on how to clean before cooking:

To clean crab before cooking, lay each crab on its back and place the cutting edge of a sharp knife with just enough force to crack the shell at the upper edge.

The crab will be stunned and offer no further resistance.

Remove the abdomen flap and, if you are still on the water, retain for proof of sex.

Grasp all the legs and claw on one side with one hand and the legs and claw on the other side with the other hand.

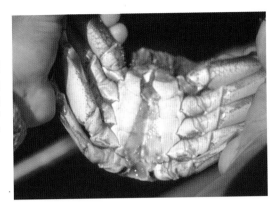

Fold both halves together and . . .

. . . remove the back.

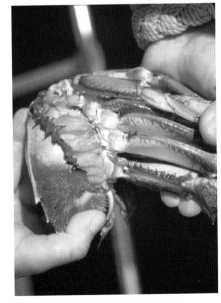

29

If you are still on the water, retain the back for proof of legal size.

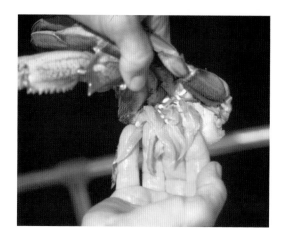

Remove the gills and discard.

Remove the loose shell fragments and entrails.

Rinse the remaining bits of intestinal matter by vigorously sloshing in water.

Here is your cleaned crab half, ready to cook. This is much more sanitary then cooking whole, and you can put more crabs in the same size pot.

One cup of rock salt per gallon of fresh water closely simulates the salinity of natural salt water. Add garlic powder to taste to the cooking water.

Bring water to full boil, add crab halves, bring back to a boil, and cook 15-18 minutes.

Have a cold water slush ready to place the cooked crab in to quickly stop the cooking.

If cooked in fresh water, the meat will be very white and the flavor quite bland. It is best if they are cooked in the same water in which they are caught, if that water is clean. Fresh water can meet the salinity of natural saltwater if one cup of rock salt is added per gallon. I like to add a touch or two of garlic powder to my cooking water. Bring the water to a boil and add your cleaned crab sections. When the water returns to a boil, time the cooking for 15 to 18 minutes. To quickly stop the cooking process, have a cold water bath ready in which to place the cooked sections. This step is unnecessary if you will be serving the sections immediately.

EATING: Hot crab meat is wonderful coming from the cooker. Pick the meat from the shell and dip it in drawn butter with another touch or two of garlic powder added. If you are going to use the crab in a salad, cool it in the icy slush solution first.

THE FINAL REWARD: The greatest reward in crabbing is sitting around the dining table with family and friends, eating succulent crab with your fingers, and enjoying good conversation.

Puget Sound Recreational Only, Non-Commercial & Limited Commercial Dungeness Crab Fishing Areas

The areas designated on the following three pages will usually produce the best crab fishing opportunities for the sport fisher.

The areas marked by green ▬ are open to recreational only harvest year round. Those are the best to target, and many can be accessed without a boat.

Those areas marked by blue ▬ are open for sport fishers all year but have limited access for commercial fishing November 1 through February 28.

Pink ▬ denotes areas that are recreational year round with limited commercial entry between October 15 and March 14.

The red ▬ areas may be entered by sports fishers all year, along with tribal commercial fishers, but they are off limits to non-tribal commercial activity at all times.

PLEASE NOTE: All these areas are subject to review each year, and new areas might be added. For current regulations, check the Shellfish Hotline: (360) 796-4601, Ext. 320. To enter your input about these areas or to suggest others for consideration, call the Mill Creek Regional Office at (425) 775-1331 or the Point Whitney Shellfish Lab at (360) 796-4601.

Dungeness Crab Fishing Areas: San Juan Islands

Sucia Island

Orcas Island

Westcott & Garrison Bays

Deer Harbor

Shaw Is.

Blind Bay

San Juan Island

Fisherman Bay

Lopez Island

Mud Bay

Non-Commercial Zone
Recreational All Year

Limited Commerical November 1 - February 28
Recreational All Year

Limited Commerical October 15 - March 14
Recreational All Year

Tribal Exclusive Zone
Recreational All Year

Dungeness Crab Fishing Areas: Padilla & Fidalgo Bays, North to Birch Bay

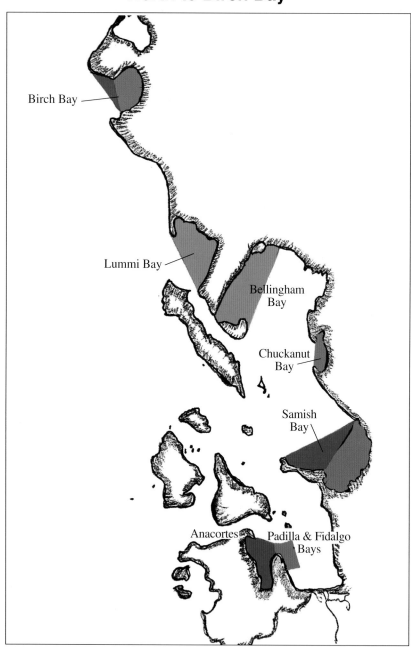

Birch Bay

Lummi Bay

Bellingham Bay

Chuckanut Bay

Samish Bay

Anacortes

Padilla & Fidalgo Bays

Dungeness Crab Fishing Areas: Possession Point, North to North Skagit & Similk Bays

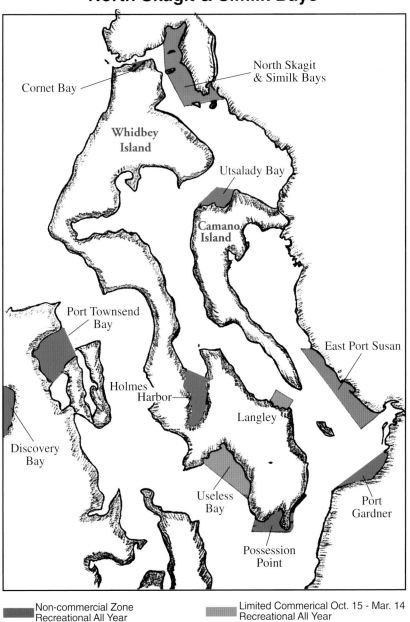

North Skagit & Similk Bays

Cornet Bay

Whidbey Island

Utsalady Bay

Camano Island

Port Townsend Bay

East Port Susan

Holmes Harbor

Langley

Discovery Bay

Useless Bay

Possession Point

Port Gardner

Non-commercial Zone
Recreational All Year

Limited Commerical Oct. 15 - Mar. 14
Recreational All Year

Limited Commerical Nov. 1 - Feb. 28
Recreational All Year

Tribal Exclusive
Recreational All Year

GREEN CRABS:
WARNING! ALIEN MONSTERS ARE COMING!

There are alien invaders headed this way that may wipe out all Dungeness crabs! Carcinus Maenas, more commonly known as "green crab," are mean and nasty and eat everything they can catch. They are particularly fond of other shellfish, especially other crabs.

On the east coast they have been wiping out the scallop industry. The town of Edgarton, Massachusetts, located on the island of Martha's Vineyard, offered a bounty of 40 cents a pound on green crab to help save the scallops. During the first five weeks, over 15,000 pounds were caught. In Maine they wiped out all the soft shell clams.

Green crab now threaten the west coast. First discovered in San Francisco Bay in 1991, they now range from Monterey Bay all the way to Vancouver Island, British Columbia. They will certainly enter Puget Sound, with no way to stop them.

These hearty crustaceans travel around the earth in the water ballast tanks of large ships, and are deposited when the ships' tanks are pumped out in harbors. They then migrate, as the female produces eggs, two million at a time. The eggs simply float out on the oceans' currents. Scientists have tracked the movement at as much as five miles per day.

U.S. Senator John Glen, D-Ohio, has sponsored legislation titled "National Invasive Species Act," which will set guidelines to regulate the discharge of ballast water from ships nationwide. This is probably a good law, but too late.

When the Oregon Department of Fish and Wildlife issued a bulletin asking crab anglers to keep and turn in all green crab they caught, people began bringing in hundreds of other species of crab, anything they saw with a green tint. Spider Crab, Hermit Crab and many three-inch Dungeness

Crab were being killed, prompting the department to rescind their request.

It was obvious that an eager but uneducated public wanted to help. All crab with a greenish tint are NOT the evil aliens; in fact not all green crab are "green." The only sure way to distinguish a green crab from all other west coast crab are the five "teeth," or spikes, on either side of the front edge of the carapace, or shell. Colors may vary during molting cycles from green to orange to red. Maximum size rarely exceeds three inches.

If you are positive that your catch is a real green crab, don't return it to the water, but keep and report it to your department of fisheries. These are a real menace and somehow must be controlled, but not by randomly killing thousands of other small species of crab.

The Green Crab is not always green. The only true distinction between these deadly invaders and every other West Coast crab species is the five "spines" on either side of the leading edge of their shell.

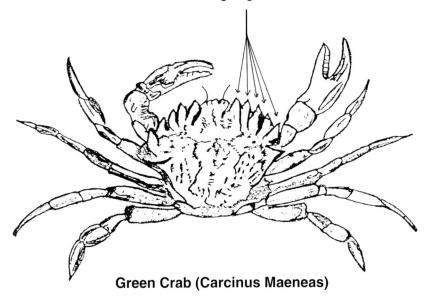

Green Crab (Carcinus Maeneas)

MUSSELS

Mussels are like bass to my family. I grew up thinking of bass as the garbage fish that plagued us when trout fishing. If we caught one, we would drop-kick it off into the bushes so it could not reproduce. After all, what were they good for? They were scaly, bony, and too little to mess with, anyhow. You see, we didn't have the right lures to catch the bigger ones. We probably didn't know bigger ones even existed.

Not until the early 60's, when military men from the South were transferred to Washington, did we discover the value of local bass. Those good old boys knew a good bass fight when they saw one. Washington bass angling exploded!

Mussels were like that. They always grew everywhere, on pilings and the undersides of docks. They could cover an entire rocky beach. At low tide they were a nuisance, making it difficult to walk from water to land, when landing your rowboat.

Although we would occasionally pick one or two out for bottomfish bait when there were no piling worms about, eating one was out of the question! Anyone knew that if you ate one from a piling it would taste like the preservative used to protect the wood. If it came from the beach it would be full

Mussels have become a delicacy enjoyed in the finest of restaurants. This Italian dish, "Cozze Ala Arancione," was prepared by Chef Dave Nelson. See page 70 for the recipe. Photo by Barry Gregg.

of grit and taste like mud, as worthless as a bass!

Only about twenty years ago did we discover what wonderful table fare these morsels could be. Although mussels had traditionally been considered a delicacy in continental Europe, we Yankees were too dumb to try eating any that might have grown in a clean environment. Although they were profuse in our marine habitat, the truth about their great flavor remained a secret. Perhaps it was intentionally kept a secret by those who knew and gathered the best for themselves; but now the secret is out. Mussels are truly a delicacy.

They thrive in saltwater, even in places where it's diluted with fresh water, such as the mouths of rivers. They grow in quiet bays and inlets, and can endure fairly high water temperatures. For these reasons, special care must be taken when harvesting. Calm harbors can accumulate high concentrations of pollutants which are not flushed out regularly. The warm waters can produce algae blooms, leading to red tide conditions.

If you find mussels growing on clean rocks, away from sand or mud, in clean cold water which has plenty of tidal flow, you could be in for a taste treat. Remember, make sure you're not on a private beach.

(WDFW)

Mussel (Mytilus Trossulus) Have oblong, blue-black or brown shells and are usually found in dense mats attached by fine threads.

Blue Mussels, also known as Bay Mussels or Mediterranean Mussels, are the best. This is the variety widely eaten in Europe, and most prolific along the west coast from Oregon to British Columbia. The only mussel species found in the Strait of Georgia, Blues will grow to a maximum length of two inches in a little over a year. Commonly found growing in clusters, the shells are oblong, blue-black or brown in color, filled with a cream or light orange meat.

Another common mussel, found only along the open

coastline where the water salinity is higher, is the California Mussel. It can grow to a length of ten inches. Its meat is orange or reddish in color. It's shell is black, and you will notice it peeling as it dries in the air between tides.

Commercial shellfish farms grow their mussels attached to fiber ropes connected to long lines and rafts. This way, the mussels never touch bottom, where their flavor could be contaminated by mud. They will also be free of sand, mud or grit. Consider this when gathering your own. They need to be clean.

TIP: Mussels must be kept alive until time to cook. Keep them cool and damp. If possible, keep them in a bag suspended in salt water. This will also "purge" them, allowing them to naturally flush out sand. A better way to purge them is to place them in a bucket of salt water and throw in a handful of corn meal. They will take in the meal while expelling their grit. The shell will be normally closed, as long as they are alive, or will quickly close when touched. Before cooking discard any that do not close, as this signifies the mussel is no longer alive. After cooking, the shell should be open. Discard any still closed after cooking.

Mussels spawn during spring months, and their meat becoms thin and watery. Since the flavor dissipates too, consider mussels off the menu from January first until June. They are a "seven month delicacy," just right for summer cruising and beach combing.

HOW TO EAT:

If you have gathered your mussels from unpolluted waters with no red tide warnings posted, you are ready to eat. (See the red tide information on pages 59-60.)

Most folks can eat about a pound of in-shell mussels per person. Maximum limits vary between states and countries, but are very liberal: 10 pounds per person, for example, in Washington; no limit in some areas of B.C. Always refer to current regulations for the locality you're in.

There is no reason to gather more than can be used for one meal, as they will be plentiful at the next low tide, and they do not store well. Keep them cool and moist, covered with a wet sack or even seaweed.

In preparation for eating, you must first get rid of their "beards." No, they don't need a shave before dinner like Uncle Ralph. They have whisker-like fibers at the shell hinge, which they use to attach to their home site. These will come off easily as you scrub the shells with a stiff brush.

Now they are ready for cooking in a variety of ways. The easiest and first step in most recipes is to put just enough water in a pan to cover the bottom, and add the mussels. Cover with a loose lid and bring the water to a boil, steaming the mussels until the shells open. After steaming, discard any shells that didn't open.

At this point the meat can be scooped out of the shells and eaten as you would steamed clams. Because their flavors are complementary, mussels and clams can be prepared together in this manner and served with melted butter.

OYSTERS

The west coast of the United States and British Columbia is awash with oyster beds containing the world's best tasting specimens. Numerous oyster companies process and annually ship more than two million gallons, or well over eight million tons, of shucked samples of these wonderful morsels to restaurants around the world. They become menu items, satisfying discriminating palates in the form of Oysters Rockefeller, oyster stew, fried oysters and in the form of many other recipes to be found in this book.

Oysters can be the gold at the end of the rainbow for boaters, or the bounty of the beach for land lovers. But when you encounter a cluster of the shell-encased entrees fit for royalty, there are certain things one must consider.

By 1920, Washington's tide flats had been picked clean of native "Olympic Oysters," because of the tremendous demand of San Francisco restaurants, which began with the 1849 Gold Rush. Harvesting practices did not consider how oysters reproduce.

Let's look at the life cycle of oysters, so we will know better how to find them and how to protect their communities.

Oysters are bisexual. They all begin life as males, and after about four years, become female for the first time. Thereafter, they alternate between producing eggs and sperm. Occasionally one can be found nurturing both eggs and sperm. Usually, an oyster is in one cycle or the other.

In the summer something within an oyster causes it to become sexually aroused. It surely has to do with the sun high overhead at just the right angle, and the flow of summer tides which aren't too strong, but just fast enough to carry eggs and sperm together and deposit them along the nearby beaches.

When conditions are just right, millions of microscopic eggs are released, triggering a response from the "males" to release gallons of sperm. When the eggs are fertilized they become "spat," also known as "seed." The spat then floats and swims, using tiny, hair-like cilia as motor power to push themselves about. An extremely high percentage of the spat will be consumed by jellyfish, starfish and other predators, or will simply float out into deep waters. After about 18 days, the remaining spat will have grown a thin shell.

While growing the shell, the emerging sea life will produce a bit of glue. At this time it could be seen as an oyster under a microscope, and is known as a "set." It is ready to find a home for life. It will attach itself to some firm object at or slightly below sea level during the time between high and low tide. In an environment of sunlight, sun warmth, and a cleansing tidal flow which will also supply food, the oyster will flourish. Favorite places for attaching are on other oyster shells lying on the beach. This is a reason for shucking your oysters on the beach, leaving the shells where you found them. More on that later.

The oysters immediately begin to grow, and are soon visible to the naked eye. By the first winter, the shell will have hardened, and each oyster will begin its first dormant period. During dormancy its growth slows, but this is also the time when mature oysters are most flavorful. Oysters are edible during any month of the year, but their flavor and condition are best when temperatures are lowest, and the oysters are not in a spawning or growth cycle.

Pacific oyster
Crassotrea gigas
Irregular, chalky-white shell. Often found in groups attached to one another or a solid object. (WDFW)

During the first four years, all oysters are in the male stage, and the majority grow to an adult size of four to five inches. After the first year, the shell becomes thicker and the meat becomes the most flavorful. "Shooters," oysters eaten raw and served on a half shell, are always two to three inches long. After an oyster reaches four inches, it is still good for frying, broiling, or other methods of cooking, but it is too large for eating raw. Really large oysters of five inches or more should be chopped up and used in stews.

WHERE TO FIND OYSTERS:

There are two types of oysters along the west coast of North America: the native "Olympia" and the imported "Pacific" variety. Olympics are seldom over one and a half inches long, while any larger oysters will probably be the Pacific variety, which can grow to seven inches across.

Olympic oysters can be found in waters from California to Alaska, glued to smooth rocks and the undersides of large boulders. They are usually attached along their full length, making them very difficult to remove. It is easier to open them while they are still attached to their home rock, rather than trying to remove them. But that is not an easy task either. It's hard to believe these fast growing bivalves were almost harvested into extinction in the years between 1850 and 1900.

Their small size and the difficulty of harvesting Olympic oysters prompted the importation of Pacific oysters from Japan, beginning in 1905 with a planting in Samish Bay, near Bellingham, Washington. Since then, they have been introduced in Tomales Bay, Humbolt Bay, and Drakes Bay, California, and along the Oregon coast, in Willapa Harbor, Greys Harbor, and throughout Puget Sound in Washington, as well as along the British Columbia and Southeastern Alaska shorelines. Considering their prolific reproduction and their migratory patterns of drifting with the tides, it's no surprise that oysters can be found along the entire west coast.

The concern in harvesting oysters is that you gather them in an environmentally safe location, during the best time periods, making sure to stay on public beaches. Pacific Oysters are always found in the intertidal zone, between high and low tide levels. This is because only the surface waters are warm enough to create sets and for their survival. If they wash into deeper water, or are discarded overboard, they can survive but will probably be eaten by starfish or other predators.

SAFE PLACES:

Oysters are the water filters of the seas. They are very efficient at removing impurities from water, so you want to make sure no pollutants are being discharged near your oyster beds. Watch for sewers or septic tank outfalls, and do not collect oysters near a marina or an area of summer homes. Many times they will not have adequate sewer systems. An area where boats regularly moor can be another source of serious pollution.

I saw an extremely interesting illustration of the efficiency of oysters as water filters which was presented by the Washington Department of Fisheries. An equal amount of harmless algae was placed in three aquarium tanks, turning the water a murky green. One had no oysters, one had six and the third had a dozen.

Within a few hours the murkiness of the waters had dissipated according to the number of oysters present. The tank with twelve oysters was crystal clear, the one with six was clearing, but the one with no oysters was even murkier.

Constantly gathering food, a single oyster will pump more then 100 gallons of water through it's shell each day! The filtering of the gills is non-selective. While removing nutritious plankton, they also separate bacteria, silt and chemicals from the water.

The material ingested is a concentration of what is in the water. Oysters are used by biologists to sample water quality. After oysters have been placed in a bay for 24 hours, scientific examination can reveal what contaminants are present. Be careful where you gather oysters. You will be eating whatever is in the water.

SAFE TIMES: Oysters are good for eating all year, but some times are better than others. It's an old wives tale that you should not eat shellfish during months without the letter "r," but it leads to a warning worth heeding. Those are the summer months of May, June, July and August. This is when improperly stored shellfish can most easily spoil, higher levels of pollutants may be present, and one may encounter "red tides." Red tides occur when increased sunlight, higher water temperatures and nutrients combine to produce a population explosion of plankton, often turning the water brown or red. These occurrences are called "blooms" and can be highly toxic. Although not all blooms are toxic, all do affect the flavor of oysters. Never eat an oyster when a bloom is present.

Another consideration during this time of year is the spawning cycle. The water temperature must be above 50° Fahrenheit at the bed,and this usually happens in late July or August. The flavor of the meat diminishes a week or so before the oyster reproduces, and the meat is thin and watery for about three weeks after spawning.

One of the hardest decisions in gathering oysters is where to do it. When beach combing or cruising, you'll see many oyster beds during low tide, but determining which are on public beaches can be tough. Many deserted looking beaches containing oyster or clam beds are privately owned. Always look for "NO TRESPASSING" signs, and obey them.

So now you've found a bed of oysters that you are reasonably sure are not on private property. You have checked up and down the bay for any sources of contamination, and it's not spawning time. You are ready to partake of a culinary delight! Remember, the smaller are the better tasting, and the larger are the best spawners.

If you plan to barbecue your catch, you will need a bag or bucket for your collection. If you will be opening your treasure before cooking, it's best to do so on the beach where the oysters were found, and you will need a clean bucket or a bowl with a lid. You will also need a shucking knife, and you will need a hammer, or suitable prying tool. Some places, such as Washington state, restrict the use of hammers.

If the oyster is attached to small pebbles or rocks, the whole mass can be picked up, and the rocks easily knocked off. Many times several individual oysters can be gathered and separated from the same mass. If they are crowded together, they will usually be attached only at their hinges, and can easily be broken apart by gentle tapping with your tool. If they are glued flat to a big rock, they are best opened in place, as it may be impossible to dislodge them without breaking the shell.

Opening oysters, called "shucking," is difficult but with practice can become quite simple. There are annual oyster shucking contests where professional shuckers routinely win by opening a dozen in less then one minute. The real art of the contest is opening them without cutting the meat. The meat of "oysters on the half-shell," which you might order in a restaurant, or those you would purchase at the supermarket, must not be damaged by a cut. Oysters damaged when opened by processors are called "cuts," and are much less valuable.

In order to open oysters without nicking the meat, we first must know what lies inside the shell. The lower half shell is usually more rounded and extends beyond the flatter upper half of the oyster. The hinge will be at the small end, with the shell opening at the larger, more rounded end. The meat will be lying in the rounded lower shell with a strong adductor muscle attached to the lower shell, and a weaker adductor muscle attached to the upper shell. These muscles are used by the oyster to keep the shell closed. One of these muscles needs to be cut cleanly to open the oyster, and then the other severed to remove the meat.

A special knife is made for this process, and it is important to use it for safety and convenience. It has a handle large enough for you to grip easily and to control the strong, stubby, rounded blade. The tip of the knife should be sharp and thin enough to slip between the lips of the shells. A heavy leather glove should be worn on the hand which will be used to hold the oyster. You can protect yourself from an inevitable slip of the knife by wearing a workman's cloth backed leather glove.

Hold the oyster in your off hand, rounded side down, and the knife in your strong hand. I find it easier to steady the oyster on a table or other firm surface with my off hand. Attack the shell from the side, about mid length. Slip the knife between shell halves and force the blade downward, under the meat, to sever the lower adductor muscle. This motion can be easily controlled by starting the blade between the shells, aiming downward, and then lifting the whole oyster a few inches off the table and slamming it back down. Ladies to whom I've taught this method find it takes much less strength to penetrate the shell with the knife.

A sweep with the blade will sever the lower muscle, allowing the shell to open. Another sweep along the upper shell will release the meat. An easier method of opening the oyster is by baking or barbecuing just long enough to open the shell a crack. Then it can easily be opened all the way with a table knife. Whichever way you do it, you should wind up with a clean uncut morsel, ready to be eaten raw or prepared in a number of different ways.

Size should be considered when deciding how to prepare your oysters. Extra small (10 to 12 in an 8 once container) or small (7 to 9 per 8 ounce) can be served raw, but any larger oysters should always be cooked for the best culinary results. Medium oysters (5 or 6 per 8 ounce) are quite tasty, but should be chopped and fried or used in stews.

Since smaller means better eating, an oyster two to three inches in length will be best. These will be the extra small to small specimens. When an oyster reaches four inches or more, the internal organs become so large that the texture is impaired.

After shucking your catch, the shells should be left upon the beach from which they were gathered. The spat will be attached to them (remember this reproduction stage), but there may also be parasites hostile to oysters. There are a number of tiny parasites which attach themselves to oyster shells, and although they do not affect human consumption, can be quite deadly to the oysters. One of the most common parasites, for example, is a snail-like creature called a "drill," because it can burrow through the shell and eat the contents. These parasites can be spread from contaminated beds to healthy ones through human transportation. So leave the shells where you found them.

Since oysters can be gathered only during reasonably low tides, you may want to store a few for tomorrow's dinner. They can be kept alive by keeping them cool and moist. Do not allow them to stand in water, as the oxygen will be used up and they will suffocate. They also do not like fresh water, so don't let them be rained upon. The best way is to store them in an open mesh container submerged in sea water. Hang it from a dock or your boat. Stored this way, they will last several weeks. Otherwise, keep them in the shade and covered by sea water-moistened burlap bags. A partially opened shell indicates a dead oyster, and should be discarded. Since oysters are best when fresh, you may want to harvest only enough for one meal. Leave the rest for the next low tide expedition. Bag limits vary, but usually are 15 to 18 per day, with a two day maximum possession limit. Some area restrictions require that the oysters be opened on the beach, with shells left behind, and shellfish licenses are always required for each person. Check your local regulations.

HOW TO EAT YOUR "SHOOTERS:" There are many great recipes for preparing oysters for the table. The first is the simplest and easiest. Just eat them raw. Restaurant menus will refer to this as "oysters on the half shell," or maybe "shooters." Only the smallest oyster is best eaten in this manner. The larger ones will have good flavor, but the internal organs are big enough to discourage most folks from wanting to eat them. Raw oysters should be thoroughly chewed to enjoy maximum flavor. If you swallow one whole, you miss the best flavor, and the experience is not unlike swallowing a raw egg. YUK!

PEARLS? When chomping your oyster on the half shell, a little care should be taken not to bite the occasional pearl. Although our west coast varieties are not known for possessing gem quality pearls, it is not uncommon to find blobs of calcium with no commercial value. These blobs are dull colored and cannot be polished to any brilliance. They are a bit of a nuisance, as they have been known to cause a chipped tooth by folks munching their shooters too fast.

SHRIMP AND PRAWNS

Some call them shrimp, but they are not merely the little guys of the seas. My family call them "San Juan Lobster." I'm here to say, whatever you call Spot Prawns, they are the tastiest morsels grown in water. To put a catch of prawns in the cooking pot, it is essential to use a boat. The sea creatures we seek are going to be found in deep water, very deep water. They have been found in water up to depths of 1500 feet, but are usually caught between 200 and 400 feet. The "shrimp zone" of 40 fathoms (240 feet) is most productive.

I prefer to target the "spot shrimp," which is considered a prawn. They grow to 10 inches long, with the meat in their tails weighing in at two ounces. That's an 8 to-the-pound tail in your seafood market. Sidestripe and pink shrimp are the smaller cousins and can be caught in shallow waters, even off docks, and especially at night when most shrimp species move to shallow zones. Sidestripe Shrimp will weigh-in at 20 to 30 per pound, and Pink Shrimp will tip the scales at 60 per pound. Eating them requires a lot of shell-peeling to recover the salad-size snacks.

The tastiest morsel living beneath the sea is the Spot Prawn with tail meat weighing up to 8 tail per pound. Note the large white spots on its back.

We need to understand more about the different species in order to know how and where to catch them. Shrimp have a definite pattern of daily migration, which all sport shrimpers should keep in mind. Prawns and shrimp migrate into deep waters by day and move into shallow waters by night. Tests have shown that spot prawns concentrate in waters of 160 to 360 feet deep by day, but are found in 60 to 160 feet of water at night.

Sidestripe are the largest shrimp along the northwest coast. They are commonly found with their spot prawn cousins by night and day. Pink Shrimp, however, are caught in trawl nets in deep water, but swim toward the surface to feed at night and during extremely overcast days. Pinks are also found 12 to 20 miles offshore, and are a major part of commercial trawl fishing.

A nice catch of sidestripe shrimp, weighing in at 20-30 shrimp per pound.

I prefer to use pots with a 7/8" mesh opening, making them legal for use anywhere, including Washington's Hood Canal. We are only going after the big spot prawns, and there is less water drag when retrieving these pots than there is with finer mesh gear. Whatever size mesh you use, secure plenty of weight inside them, 7 to 10 pounds minimum. Use plenty of line, at least 100 feet longer than the depth, which will compensate for tidal pull and wave action. Secure an ounce of weight 10 feet from your yellow identification buoy, to keep it from floating up into somebody's propeller. That buoy must have your name and address on it.

As in so many areas, technology is changing the type of bait we use for shrimping. For many years the bait of choice has been the cheap and greasy fish flavored cat food. Puss-n-Boots Fisherman's Platter was actually formulated for use as shrimp bait in Hood Canal. Now a more powerful blend is being marketed in a pellet form, for use in plastic containers with small holes. Commercial shrimpers swear by this product. If you stick with the cat food, remove and properly stow the label, to prevent littering; then perforate the can along the sides and at both ends. Whatever bait you use, you want the scent to disperse quickly, attracting shrimp.

I soak my gear for 20 minutes, and then pull up one pot to see if any shrimp are present. If not, I move to another spot. Using my depth finder, I try to set my pots about 40 fathoms deep on the high point of an underwater ridge. This is the best place for the bait to leave a scent trail. The weight you attach is important for holding on the exposed ridge. Ten pounds of weight is not excessive, but anywhere from 7 to15 pounds may be used. The best shrimping time is from an hour before to an hour after a slack tide, or when there is little tidal flow. During stronger tidal flows the shrimp hide behind structures for protection from being swept away. For this reason you would also want to place your gear behind some protection.

Rules, regulations and limits vary, and in some states are very complicated. Before leaving, refer to the local shellfish regulations for the area you will be targeting. For example, Hood Canal's season is not announced until May, for a 3 to 6 day opening, Wednesdays and Saturdays only, and then only from 9 a.m. to 1 p.m., with an 80 prawn limit.

COOKING: Shrimp will live several hours in a bucket covered with the same seawater in which they were caught. Therefore, they should be protected and cooked fresh.

The best method is to boil them in salt water, either the water in which they were caught, if it is clean, or by adding one cup of rock salt to each gallon of fresh water used. I always add garlic powder (to taste).

Bring the water to a full boil and add the shrimp. When the water resumes boiling, time the cooking carefully from five to eight minutes. Longer cooking will produce a firmer texture. Remove from the water and immediately cool to prevent overcooking. (Place in a container of ice water.) To eat, peel away the shell and remove the streak of dark entrails from the back. Some shrimp will not have this streak. They are a wonderful treat, eaten as they are, or used in a variety of hot or cold dishes. See the recipes section for preparation suggestions.

TOXINS

Clams, oysters, mussels and, to a lesser extent, crab all act as water filters, gathering in and retaining anything suspended in the water in which they live. They concentrate hazardous toxins within their systems. For that reason, it is important to ensure that the water from which you gather them is clean, and free of both pollutants and toxins.

The most common toxin is referred to as "red tide." This condition occurs when air and water temperatures rise, while the winds and tides become calm. This causes an organism, Gymnodinium breve, to massively increase, to the extent that the water actually turns a reddish-brown. This is called a "bloom," and in itself it is not harmful to humans. As shellfish absorb water and filter it, they retain dangerous concentrations of this hazardous material. The rise in this algae-like organism does not have to be visible to become harmful, especially to elderly people.

Other toxins which do not discolor the water can become problems, also. There are 20 toxins responsible for paralytic shellfish poisoning known as "PSP." All are part of a group of molecular acids which are harmless until concentrated in shellfish. Amnesic shellfish poisoning, "ASP," is another toxin caused by an unusual amino acid, "domoic acid."

Ingestion of contaminated shellfish results in a wide variety of symptoms depending on the toxin present, it's concentration in the shellfish, and the amount of contaminated shellfish consumed. In the case of PSP, the effects are predominantly neurological and include tingling, burning, numbness, drowsiness, incoherent speech and respiratory paralysis.

Less severe are symptoms related to ASP poisoning, which may be observed as a general mild gastrointestinal disorder. Nausea, vomiting, diarrhea, and abdominal pain accompanied by chills, headache and fever can ruin a good dinner which was contaminated with ASP. Symptoms of these poisonings may occur anywhere from a few minutes to a couple of hours after eating.

All these toxins are rare in northwest waters, due to the cooler climate and colder water temperatures. To avoid them, call the local **Red Tide Hotline**, before gathering your shellfish.

Write down your local red tide hotline number in your tide guide:

California Department of Health Services, shellfish information line: (510) 540-2605.

Oregon Department of Fish and Wildlife, marine region information: Newport (541) 867-4741, Charleston (541) 888-5515, or Astoria (503) 325-2462.

Washington State Department of Health, toxin/PSP hotline: 800-562-5632.

B.C. Fisheries and Oceans, shellfish and red tide update: (604) 666-3169.

Another important number for Washington residents is the Shellfish Rule Change Hotline: (360) 796-3215.

OTHER TOLERABLE EDIBLES

There are some creatures living in our waters that look obnoxious and are repulsive to touch. When you get past all that, some are gourmet delicacies and others quite edible if one is hungry enough. I always wonder, who was the first starving person to tear into an artichoke and discover the delicious heart?

ABALONE

For the foreseeable future, the northern Abalone (Haliotis Kamschatkana) will have to yield to its cousins in California to satisfy the appetite for this de-
lectable shellfish. Surveys have revealed a continuing decline in the number and size of northern abalone, leading to a complete ban on all harvest. In Washing-ton State, I'm told, that ban will likely last into the year 2010.

Abalone
(Haliotis Kamschatkana)

OCTOPUS

Northwest waters are home to the largest octopus in size and number in the world. This shy and retiring creature has erroneously been made the villain in countless Holly-wood movies. In real life, the last thing it wants to do is at-tack humans. This mollusk (Octopus Dofleini) can measure up to twelve feet in diameter and can weigh 120 pounds.

Octopus (Octopus Dofleini)

Most of its edible meat comes from the arms, or tentacles, and has a clam-like flavor. It is usually "chewy-tough," requiring tenderizing as a large clam would.

Octopus are usually found hiding in caves in rocky areas by scuba divers, but occasionally one will attach itself to a crab or shrimp trap for a quick trip to the surface when the trap is pulled. It is also not uncommon for one to attach to an anchor, for a ride to the surface while the boat gets underway.

It can become a ticklish situation when you get an octopus on deck. What do you do with it? It can move through any opening large enough for its hard beak to pass through. I once brought a small one aboard in a shrimp trap, from which it quickly escaped and took refuge under a boat seat. As we turned our attention to landing more shrimp traps, we didn't notice the 'pus sneaking up the back of the seat until it came "eye-to-eye" with my five-year-old son. With a yelp and within the blink of an eye, my son was perched upon the windshield. Then the really loud sounds began! To this day, my grown son HATES octopus!

Octopus must be caught with hands or instruments like shrimp traps which do not penetrate the octopus. When an octopus is caught with a hook and line, it can be kept.

SCALLOPS

Pink or spiny scallops (Chalmys) are common in northern waters, but usually the only evidence are empty shells washed up on beaches. These unique, clam-like swimming bivalves jet through the water by quickly closing a valve and ejecting a stream of water through a small hole. Large schools of scallops entertain scuba divers by resembling a cloud of sets of dentures opening and closing, while moving erratically backward. They are harvested almost exclusively by commercial trawl nets in deep water, but can occasionally be found in

Spiny Scallop (top row)
Pink Scallop (bottom row)
(WDFW)

Rock Scallop (left) &
Weathervane Scallop (right)
(WDFW)

shallows at low tide. Catching them can be a challenge. Got a butterfly net?

Rock scallops (Hinnites Multirugosus) present another challenge for sportsmen. Living below the low tide mark in rocky areas, rock scallops may be completely camouflaged with tube worms and barnacles. When found, they are extremely good eating. This is an unfamiliar shellfish due to the difficulty of harvesting it.

Weathervane scallops (Pecten Caurinus) are beautiful, tasty and also unfamiliar. They can grow to nine inches across, but are never found in less then 60 feet of water. Found on muddy or sandy bottoms at great depths, they are usually only taken as an incidental catch by commercial drag nets tilling the ocean bottom.

SEA CUCUMBER

Here's one that even hard-core mariners have a hard time dealing with. The sea cucumber (Parastichopus Californicus) is ugly, with a wart covered reddish skin, and slimy, squishy feel. When lifted out of the water, it will relieve itself with a stream of water that has been trapped inside, and deflate in a truly obscene fashion. It will then

Sea Cucumber
(Parastichopus Californicus)

twitch and squirm when you slit it from end to end, like the huge worm it really is.

After it is laid open, five bands of muscle will be seen running lengthwise. Peel the muscle away from the skin and dice. The flavor is very rewarding, much like that of scallops, with the tender meat tasting good sautéed or in chowder. Sea cucumber are commonly brought to the surface after being snagged from a reef on a bottomfishing hook, or after being found in the deeper tidal pools when one is wading on rocky beaches.

SEA URCHINS

The sea urchin really tests the hunger of beach combers and divers. These underwater pincushions come in three varieties: red urchin (Strongylocentrotus), found in the San Juan Islands; green urchin (S. Drobachiensis), abundant in Puget Sound; and purple urchin (S. Purpuratus), common in tide pools and shallow water.

Many people cannot get past the sight and feel of these creatures, but they are one of Washington State's most widely exported seafood delicacies. Divers harvest multi-millions of pounds annually for export, mainly to Japanese markets.

Sea Urchins

Encased within the heavy shell, which is covered by hundreds of sharp spines, are five sections of tiny, yellowish-orange, egg-like roe, the edible portion. After cracking open the shell, this roe can be eaten raw with a spoon (the preferred method), or slightly cooked, breaded and spread upon crackers.

Shelf life, after being removed from the water, is measured in hours. Urchin dive boats are distinguished by the air compressors mounted on their decks which are connected to long air lines enabling divers to stay down for long periods. They can be seen delivering catches to docks in Friday Harbor, on San Juan Island. Waiting trucks drive the catch onto ferries and hurry to Sea-Tac Airport to meet waiting aircraft, which fly the harvest to Japan.

SQUID

The good news is we have no giant, submarine grabbing á la Hollywood type of squid in the northwest. The bad news is that all our squid are less than 6 to 10 inches long, and are more popularly used as bait for other aquatic species. Schools of squid (Loligo Opalescens) can be seen swimming near the surface, many times followed by schools of salmon seeking a meal. When competing with the salmon, anglers are allowed to use a baitfish jig consisting of not more then 4 squid lures, a herring rake, or a hand dip net.

Hardcore squid anglers show up at Puget Sound docks at night, when schools of squid are in. They arrive with power generators in tow for operating bright halogen lights, which are used to attract the squid to their waiting lures. Current daily limits are 5 quarts or 10 pounds. After the squid are cleaned and prepared for eating, you may use any calamari recipe.

Squid (Loligo Opalescens)

RECIPES: IT'S TIME TO EAT

The recipes listed here are all simple to prepare requiring a minimum of condiments. They can be used in a campsite over a fire or campstove, aboard a boat equipped with simple cooking equipment, or there are even a couple for the microwave, at home or aboard.

SERVING TIP:
Pack hot, cooked Basmati or other white rice into a well buttered ring mold. Let it stand a few minutes to set up, then remove the mold on a serving platter. Fill the hollow with shrimp/prawn tails, crab legs, fried clams or oysters, or any combination. Add your favorite vegetable for an attractive serving dish.

BEACH AND BARNYARD:
Just as fish and red meat make a popular "surf and turf" menu entree, shellfish and schnitzel are partners. Any of the following recipes can be served with a cut of pork. Bacon, chops or sausage will enhance the flavor of your favorite shellfish dinner.

CRAB NOODLE:
We saw in the crab section how to clean and cook crab and how to pick and eat them. Here's another way my family enjoys the flavor. Prepare a box of noodles and cheese, such as Noodle-Roni, per package directions. During the last minute of cooking stir in a half pound or more of shucked crab meat.

MOM'S FAMOUS CLAM FRITTERS

I first remember my mom telling the young people from the neighboring campsite at Westport, Washington, how to prepare the razor clams they had just dug. She recommended a quick and easy recipe for clam patties known as "fritters." Ingredients:

    1 cup pancake mix
    1/4 tsp. salt
    2 eggs (beaten)
    3 tbsp. milk
    1 "smidgen" (1 tbsp.) butter
    2 cup "minced" clam (We carried a small portable hand grinder for "mincing;" finely chopped will suffice.)

Blend all ingredients and form into patties in a sauté skillet. Brown both sides and serve buttered. (I like to drip a little honey on them.)

"SMOKED" RAZOR (OR ANY OTHER) CLAMS

An easy way to prepare a great tasting snack that will keep when refrigerated 2 to 3 weeks:

    15 razor clams cut in small pieces (or 40 to 50 "steamer" clam meats)
    1/2 cup oil
    3 tbsp. liquid smoke
    2 tbsp. Worcestershire sauce
    2 tbsp. lemon juice
    1 tbsp. seasoning salt
    1 tbsp. chili powder
    1 tbsp. celery salt
    1 tbsp. garlic powder

Combine and stir oil and seasonings, then add clams. Bake on a cookie sheet or shallow pan at 350° for an hour. Stir and drain frequently, saving the juices. Store clams and juice in an airtight container.

CLAM CHOWDER CLAYTON

8 slices bacon
1 onion, chopped
2 or 3 large peeled potatoes
1/2 tsp. thyme
1/2 tsp. pepper
1 can mushroom soup
1 can cream of celery soup
1 can water
1 can (13 oz.) evaporated milk
2 cans minced clams, or 1 to 1 1/2 c. fresh ground
   clams

Cut bacon into 1/4 inch pieces and fry together with onion until tender and slightly crisp. Cut potatoes into 1 inch cubes and place in pan with enough slightly salted water to cover potatoes. Boil until tender, but firm. Add drained bacon and onion. Stir in remaining ingredients and simmer on low heat.

Mix 3 tbsp. flour with enough water to make a thick paste (no lumps). Add to chowder. Cook until thickened. Add water if thinner chowder is desired. Add 1 c. parmesan cheese. Serve with French bread or rolls.

STEAMED CLAMS OR MUSSELS

Clams and mussels are usually steamed and served in the shell. Allow them to "purge" themselves of sand and grit in clean water for a couple hours. Discard any with open shells. Brush off any dirt and scrub "beards" from mussels, before placing in a large pan with an inch or two of water. I like to add a bit of garlic salt to the water. Cover and steam until shells open. Discard any shells that did not open.

Serve hot with melted garlic butter. Scoop meat out of shells with a fork and dip in butter.

MUSSELS ON THE HALF SHELL

After steaming, mussels (and large clams) can be served on a half shell. Large Blue Mussels work best for this recipe. Remove steamed meat from shells and save shells.

Finely chop 1/2 cup green onion.

Finely chop 1/2 red pepper.

Finely chop 1/2 medium yellow onion.

Juice from one lemon or 1 tbsp. concentrated lemon juice

2 tbsp. soy sauce

1 c. grated parmesan cheese

1/4 c. soft butter

Blend all ingredients well.

Place meats in half shells, sprinkle mixture over meats and broil until light brown. This takes about 10 minutes, but watch carefully not to burn them.

COZZE á LA ARANCIONE*
(Mussels ála Orange)

12 oz. bearded mussels

1 oz. butter

1/2 tsp. shallots, chopped

2 tbsp. leeks, sliced

1/8 c.Tuaca

1/4 c. fresh squeezed orange juice

1/2 c. heavy cream

3 tbsp. peeled, seeded, and chopped tomato

salt

white pepper

1/2 tsp. chopped parsley

1/4 tsp. orange zest

Sauté shallots and leeks in butter over low heat until lightly wilted, about 2 minutes. Add Tuaca, orange juice and mussels. Cover and steam. Remove mussels when opened, and keep warm. Add cream to sauce; reduce over high heat by one-third. Add tomatoes, parsley, salt, and white pepper to taste. Heat through. Pour over mussels. Sprinkle with orange zest and fresh watercress. Arrange mussels, open shell up. Do not completely cover with sauce.

* from *Celebrate 100: The Washington State Centennial Cookbook* (Romar Books Ltd./Evergreen Pacific Publishing Ltd). Recipe submitted to that 1989 centennial edition by the "il fiasco" restaurant of Bellingham, Washington.

FRIED CLAMS OR OYSTERS

1 pint of steamed clam meats or small uncooked,
    shucked oyster meats
1 c. flour
1 c. bread crumbs (optional)
2 eggs (beaten)
1/2 c. butter
salt and pepper to taste
lemon wedges

Drain clams or oysters and pat dry. Mix flour with bread crumbs if used. Combine beaten eggs with salt & pepper. Roll meats in eggs, then flour. Fry in melted butter until browned on both sides. Serve with lemon wedges.

DEEP FRIED CLAMS OR OYSTERS WITH POTATO

This recipe for frying clams or oysters will satisfy even picky eaters.

1/2 c. sour cream (milk will do)
1/4 c. flour
1/2 tsp. salt
1 egg (beaten)
2 c. finely shredded potatoes
1 pint clam or oyster meats (drained and patted dry)
enough oil for deep frying

Stir together sour cream (or milk) and seasonings, and add to beaten eggs. Add potatoes and blend thoroughly. Add clams or oysters to mixture. Heat oil to 375° in pan, wok or deep fryer. Drop mixture by large spoonfuls into hot oil. Keep morsels separated so they float freely, one layer deep. Fry until golden brown, about 2 to 3 minutes. Remove and drain on paper towels.

BARBECUED OYSTERS

Another quick and easy way to cook oysters, and by far the easiest means to open them, is on the grill or in the oven.

Simply wash your oyster shells so you are not serving sand on your plates. Lay shells on your barbecue grate or oven grill, "bowl" side down, "flat" side up. Heat until shells open, pull top off and cover with your favorite barbecue sauce.

NOTE: This is also the way to serve OYSTERS ON THE HALF SHELL, by substituting butter for the barbecue sauce and adding a dash of Tabasco sauce.

GUN CLUB OYSTER STEW

The oldest continuously operating gun club in Washington State is the North Whidbey Sportsmen's Association, in Oak Harbor. Longtime member, Harris Eloph, has been making the World's Best Oyster Stew for every January meeting for the past 20 years.

To feed 40 hungry sportsmen, Harris uses one gallon of large oysters cut into bite size portions. Prepare in a large pot with all the juice from the gallon container, along with a half pound of butter.

Heat to barely bubbling, but NOT BOILING. Turn down and simmer at least four hours, the longer the better. Harris says, "At a simmer you can't hurt it; but if you boil it, the oysters will become as tough as rubber."

That's it! No spices or other ingredients. Serve with warm, but not hot enough to scald, whole milk and butter (one gallon of milk to 1/4 pound of butter). Use a ladle to scoop a portion of stew into a bowl, then scoop an equal portion of warm milk into the bowl. Salt and pepper it to taste, and serve with "oyster crackers" or saltines.

For smaller gatherings, a quart of oysters with a quart of milk and equivalent reductions of butter portions will suffice. Remember the "secret:" simmer the oysters in their own juice with butter for as long as possible on low heat. Stir occasionally.

CIOPPINO – SEAFOOD GUMBO

1/4 c. butter (or margarine)
1 1/2 lb. clams in the shell
1 1/2 lb. cod or red snapper
2 lb. crab in the shell
3/4 lb. shrimp in shell
6 oz. large shell macaroni
2 medium onions, chopped
2 garlic cloves, pressed or minced
1/3 c. chopped parsley
2 (14 oz.) cans chicken broth
1 c. water
2 c. dry white wine
1 bay leaf
1/2 tsp. thyme leaves
1/2 tsp. rosemary leaves
2 or 3 tomatoes, chopped

Melt butter in 6 quart kettle. Add onion, garlic and parsley. Cook until onion is soft, stirring often. Mix in bay leaf, wine, thyme, rosemary, broth and water. Simmer 15 minutes.

Rinse off clam shells, cut fish into 1 inch pieces, break legs off body of crab which is cleaned, but still in the shell. Place crab legs and body, clams, noodles and fish into the kettle. Cover and simmer until noodles are done (10 minutes). Add cleaned shrimp the last 3 minutes. Add tomatoes. Mix well. Serve while hot with French bread and your favorite wine.

AVOCADO STUFFED WITH CRABMEAT

Sauce for this is made with 1/2 c. of mayonnaise, 1/2 c. of stiffly whipped cream, 1/3 c. of chili sauce and 1 tbsp. of grated onion. Mix with crabmeat and pile into half of avocado.

BAKED TOMATOES WITH CRAB STUFFING

1/2 lb. cooked, cleaned crab or 1 (7 1/2 oz.) can crab
6 medium tomatoes
1 tbsp. butter
1/4 c. chopped onion
1/2 c. chopped celery
1/4 c. chopped green pepper
1 1/2 c. coarse dry bread crumbs
1 tsp. salt
1/8 tsp. pepper
1/2 tsp. basil
Grated parmesan cheese

Drain and slice canned crab or use fresh crab, reserving 6 slices of leg piece for garnish. Cut slice from stem end of each tomato. Scoop out pulp and reserve, discarding seeds. Turn tomato shells upside down to drain. Melt butter in skillet. Add onion, celery and green pepper and sauté until tender. Chop reserved tomato pulp and add to skillet. Cook for a few minutes. Remove from heat and add bread crumbs, crab, salt, pepper and basil. Sprinkle insides of tomato shells with salt. Fill with crab mixture. Sprinkle with grated parmesan cheese, bake at 375° for 20 to 25 minutes, or until tomatoes are tender. For the last 5 minutes of baking, garnish with reserved leg pieces to heat thoroughly.

SHRIMP COCKTAIL

3/4 c. chili sauce
1/4 c. lemon juice
1 tbsp. Horseradish
1 tsp. minced onion
2 tsp. Worcestershire sauce
4 drops Tabasco sauce
Dash of salt
Shrimp (cooked and cleaned)

Combine ingredients except shrimp. Chill thoroughly. Spoon sauce into individual cocktail cups over chilled shrimp. Garnish cup by hooking several shrimp over rim of glass. Makes 1 cup of sauce.

SWEET AND SOUR SHRIMP

1/4 c. salad oil
1 c. celery, diced
1 c. green pepper, diced
2 tsp. flour
1 1/2 c. tomato juice
1/3 c. brown sugar
1/2 tsp. salt
1/4 c. lemon juice
1 tbsp. grated lemon rind
1 1/2 lb. fresh cooked shrimp
1 small can sliced pineapple

Sauté pepper, celery and onion in oil. Do not brown. Add flour and blend. Add tomato juice, sugar, salt, lemon juice and rind. Cook 5 minutes. Add shrimp and pineapple slices. Heat and serve with rice. Serves 6.

SCALLOPS SAUTÉ

1 1/2 lbs. bay scallops
Flour
6 tbsp. olive oil
1/3 c. chopped parsley
2 or 3 garlic cloves, chopped finely
salt and pepper

Thoroughly clean scallops and roll them in flour. Place in heated olive oil and cook rapidly while tossing lightly. As the scallops are cooking, add the chopped garlic and mix well. Add parsley and toss with the scallops. Serve with lemon wedges.

Variation: omit garlic and add 1 tsp. tarragon, 1 tsp. chives and parsley.

BROILED SCALLOPS

Place lightly buttered scallops on a flat baking sheet and sprinkle with salt and pepper. Broil 5 to 6 minutes or until lightly browned. Serve with lemon juice.

IN CONCLUSION

Whether you are new to the Northwest marine scene or a longtime resident, adding shellfish to your culinary experience will greatly enrich your life. Tasty nutritious dinners gathered from nearby waters can make you healthier and happier.

Any meal or snack can be enhanced by including shellfish. Most folks can eat 1/3 pound of crab meat, 15 to 20 steamer clams, a dozen small oysters in shell or one pint shucked, or one pound of shrimp meat per sitting.

When preparing shellfish, remember not to overcook shellfish or any other seafood. It will become dry and tough, if you do. Keep your cooking method and recipe simple, using a minimum of seasonings to allow the natural flavor of the shellfish to come through. When making chowder, use an amount of shellfish meat equal to the quantity of potatoes.

When gathering shellfish, only take the amount you can use for dinner. It is always best fresh, and never as good after being frozen or even refrigerated overnight. It's better to draw out the experience of gathering shellfish to another day, and again enjoy the fresh flavor.

Make your shellfish hunting a family adventure, and enjoy your healthy meal together.

APPENDIX A
Puget Sound Shellfish Site Maps*

How to Use the Maps and Indexes

The maps in this appendix identify many of the public shellfish sites around Puget Sound that offer some form of recreational opportunity. Some smaller beaches were difficult to show on maps of this scale and therefore were not included. Beaches with known boundary line or ownership problems are not listed. Maps 1-9 are two-page spreads. The northern section of each of the those maps is on the even numbered page, and the southern section on the opposite odd numbered page. All these maps contain the most current information available as of the edition of this book.

Finding a Beach

The following section of this booklet contains two indexes and 10 maps. Every beach shown has a number next to it. **However, only beaches with names are listed in the indexes**. An alphabetical index by beach name is found preceeding the maps, and a numerical index by beach number is found after the maps.

Requesting Information

Please refer to beaches by number and name when requesting information about a beach. **If you know of any beach name corrections or new beaches to be added, please contact the Washington Department of Fish and Wildlife's Point Whitney Shellfish Laboratory at 360-796-4601.**

Understanding Marine Biotoxin Closure Areas

The maps contain common landmarks used to describe closure areas on the marine biotoxin hotline. Referring to maps in this appendix will help you identify closure areas.

Color Codes of the Maps

The environmental health of certain areas are color coded green, blue, yellow, and red on the maps. These areas have been adapted from commercial growing area classifications and give a generalized representation of the health of an area. Not all beaches within a colored area have been classified. These area health classifications are for bivalve shellfish only and are not intended for other types of shellfish harvested from the beach, such as crab.

Green color indicates areas that are generally approved for commercial and recreational shellfish harvest. However, a beach within a

* Reprinted from *Public Shellfish Sites of Puget Sound*, a booklet originally prepared by the Washington Department of Fisheries in 1989 and then revised in 1999 through the combined efforts of Washington departments of Health, Fish & Wildlife, Natural Resources, & Ecology; the Parks & Recreation Commission; the Puget Sound Water Quality Action Team; the Bremerton-Kitsap Co. Health District; the N.W. Indian Tribes, and the University of Washington Sea Grant Program. The maps were created by Derry Suther and Randy Butler.

green area that is unclassified (without a symbol by the beach) by the Washington Department of Health has not had a site specific evaluation. Harvesters should inquire with their local health department.

Blue color indicates areas that are conditionally open for commercial and recreational harvest. This means that under certain conditions, usually excessive rainfall, or seasonal boat useage, these areas have the potential to become contaminated. Harvesters should inquire with their local health department prior to harvesting on all beaches with this classification.

Yellow color indicates areas where harvesting is not advised due to the proximity to urban areas. Beaches in these areas are exposed to a number of sources with the potential for contamination from chemical and bacterial contaminants.

Red color indicates areas that are closed for commercial and recreational harvest. These areas have known contamination sources such as failing onsite sewage systems, agricultural runoff, marinas, and sewage treatment plant outfalls.

Unclassified areas of the maps without color have not been evaluated by the Washington Department of Health.

Because of changing conditions the accuracy of the maps cannot be guaranteed. Contact the local health department prior to harvesting on ANY beach.

Beach Index Abbreviations
CP – County Park
HBR – Harbor
HD – Head
IS – Island
LT – Little
NWR – National Wildlife Refuge
PK – Park
PT – Point
REC – Recreation
RES – Reserve
RKS – Rocks
USFS – United States Forest Service

Beach Index — Alphabetical

Beach Index — Alphabetical (cont.)

Beach Index — Alphabetical (cont.)

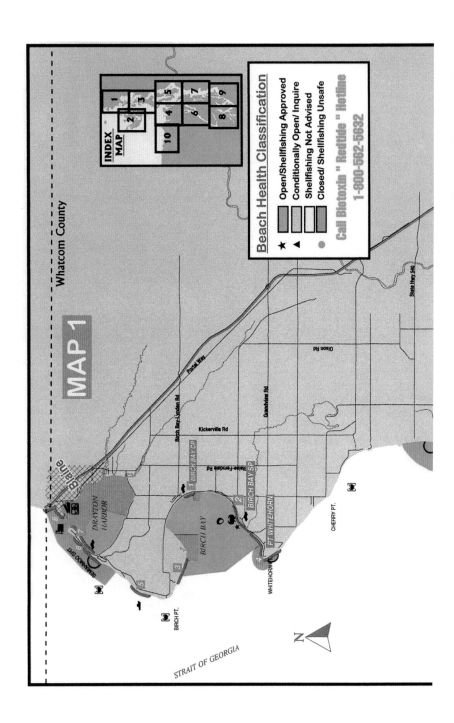

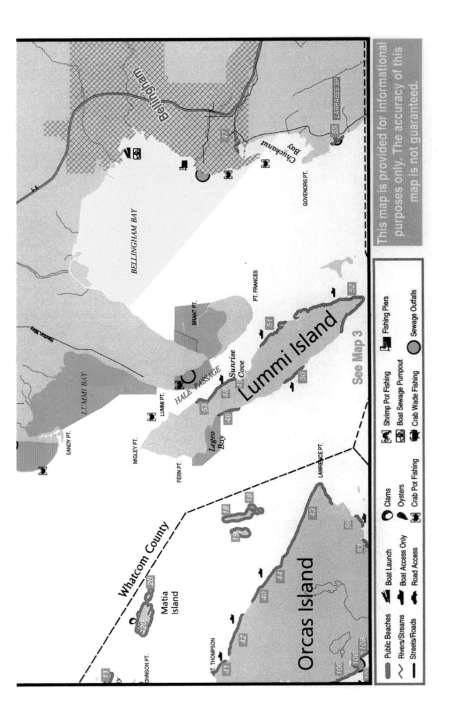

This map is provided for informational purposes only. The accuracy of this map is not guaranteed.

Legend:
- Public Beaches
- Rivers/Streams
- Streets/Roads
- Boat Launch
- Boat Access Only
- Road Access
- Clams
- Oysters
- Crab Pot Fishing
- Shrimp Pot Fishing
- Boat Sewage Pumpout
- Crab Wade Fishing
- Fishing Piers
- Sewage Outfalls

Bellingham

BELLINGHAM BAY

Chuckanut Bay

LARRABEE SP

GOVERNORS PT.

PT. FRANCES

BRANT PT.

LUMMI BAY

SANDY PT.

MIGLEY PT.

LUMMI PT.

HALE PASSAGE

Sunrise Cove

Lageo Bay

FERN PT.

Lummi Island

See Map 3

LAWRENCE PT.

Whatcom County

Matia Island

JOHNSON PT.

ST. THOMPSON

Orcas Island

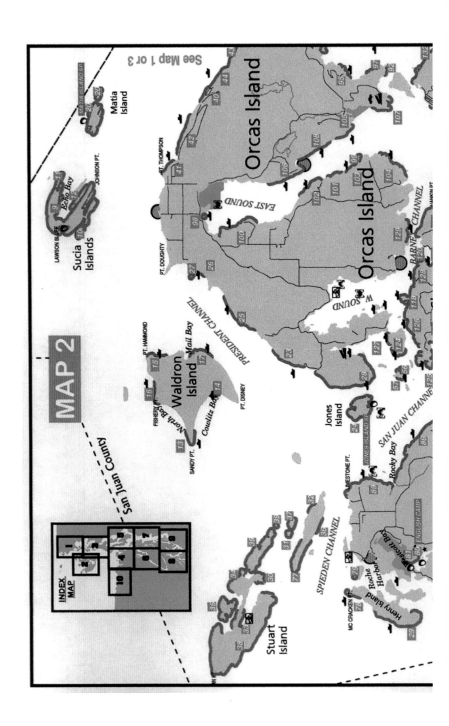

MAP 2

See Map 1 or 3

Matia Island

Orcas Island

Orcas Island

Echo Bay

Sucia Islands

San Juan County

Waldron Island

President Channel

East Sound

W. Sound

Rainel Channel

Jones Island

San Juan Channel

Spieden Channel

Stuart Island

Roche Harbor

Henry Island

Rocky Bay

English Camp

INDEX MAP

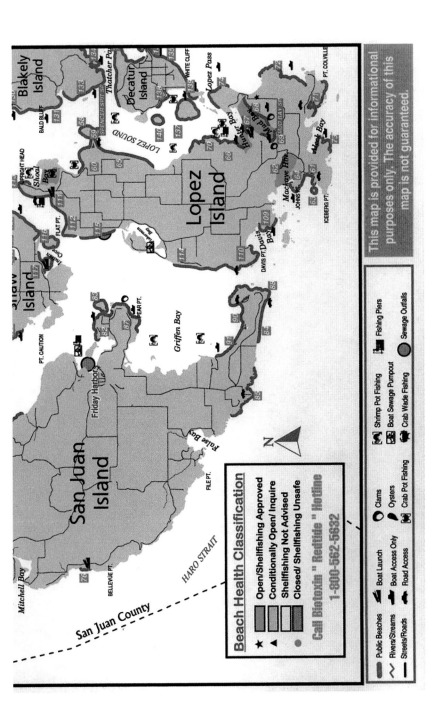

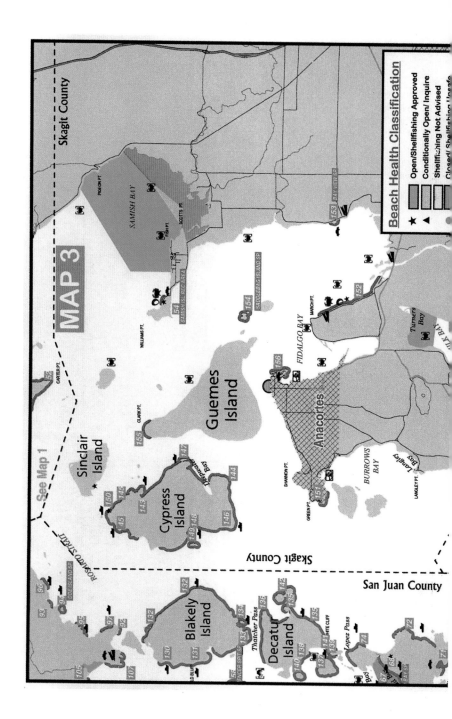

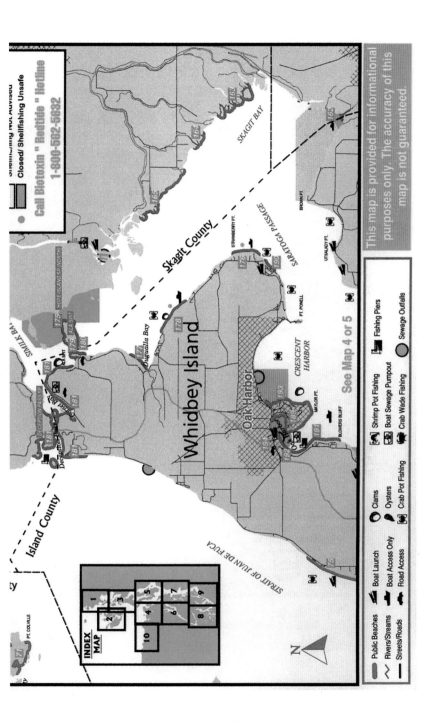

Call Biotoxin "Redtide" Hotline
1-800-562-5632

● Closed/ Shellfishing Unsafe

This map is provided for informational purposes only. The accuracy of this map is not guaranteed.

Island County

Skagit County

Smilk Bay

Skagit Bay

SARATOGA PASSAGE

Whidbey Island

Oak Harbor

CRESCENT HARBOR

Oliguuila Bay

DECEPTION PASS SP

Deception Pass

STRAIT OF JUAN DE FUCA

PT. COLVILLE

BROWN PT.

UTSALADY PT.

PT. POWELL

MAYLOR PT.

BLOWERS BLUFF

STRAWBERRY PT.

HOPE ISLAND SP NORTH

See Map 4 or 5

INDEX MAP

1 2 3 4 5 6 7 8 9 10

N

Public Beaches
Rivers/Streams
Streets/Roads

Boat Launch
Boat Access Only
Road Access

Clams
Oysters
Crab Pot Fishing

Shrimp Pot Fishing
Boat Sewage Pumpout
Crab Wade Fishing

Fishing Piers
Sewage Outfalls

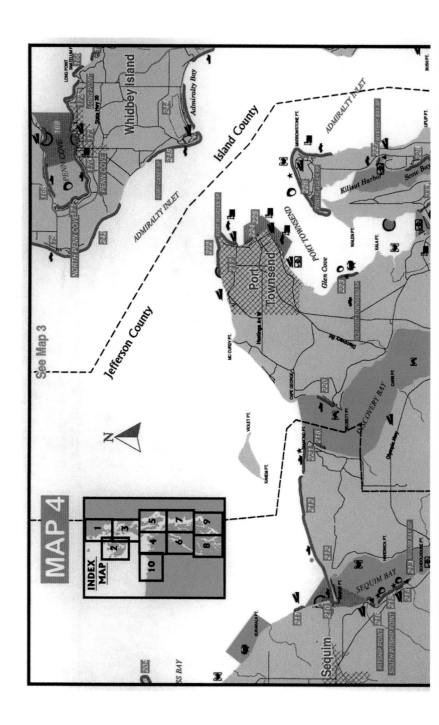

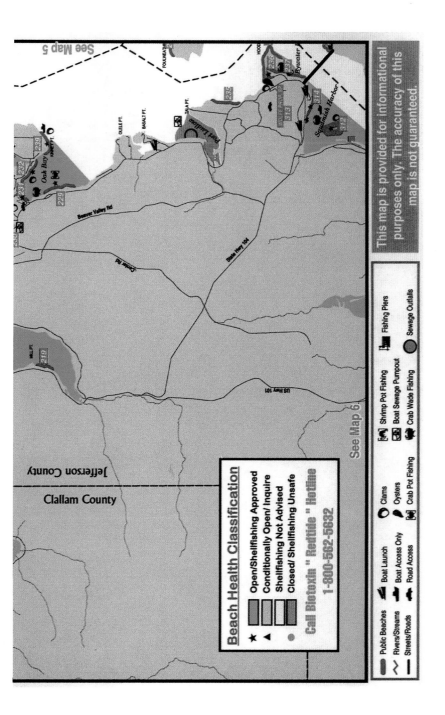

See Map 5

Jefferson County

Clallam County

Oak Bay

Beaver Valley Rd

Center Rd

State Hwy 104

US Hwy 101

Squamish Harbor

Port Ludlow

MILL PT.

OLELE PT.

BASALT PT.

ZELA PT.

FOULWEATHER

Bywater

See Map 6

Beach Health Classification

★ Public Beaches
◀ Rivers/Streams
— Streets/Roads

Boat Launch
Boat Access Only
Road Access

Clams
Oysters
Crab Pot Fishing

Shrimp Pot Fishing
Boat Sewage Pumpout
Crab Wade Fishing

Fishing Piers
Sewage Outfalls

Open/Shellfishing Approved
Conditionally Open/ Inquire
Shellfishing Not Advised
Closed/ Shellfishing Unsafe

★ ◀ ●

Call Biotoxin " Redtide " Hotline
1-800-562-5632

89

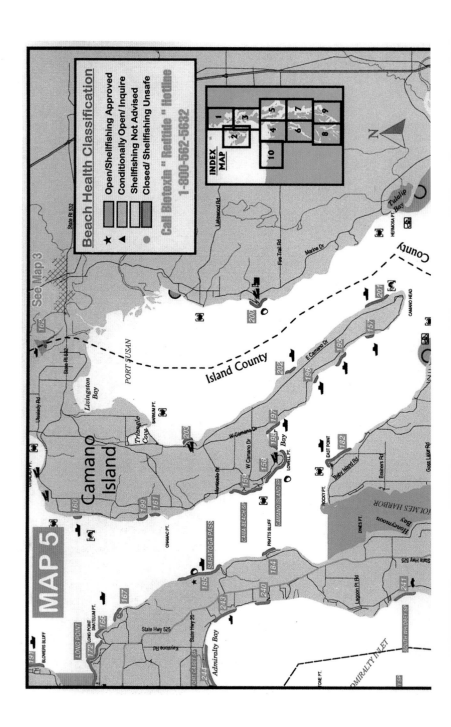

MAP 5

Camano Island

Beach Health Classification

★ Open/Shellfishing Approved
◄ Conditionally Open/ Inquire
● Shellfishing Not Advised
● Closed/ Shellfishing Unsafe

**Call Biotoxin " Redtide " Hotline
1-800-562-5632**

INDEX MAP

1 2 3 4 5 6 7 8 9 10

N

See Map 3

State Rt 532

Lakewood Rd

Fire Trail Rd

Marine Dr

Hermosa Pt.

Tulalip Bay

PORT SUSAN

Island County

County

CAMANO HEAD

201

157

195

E Camano Dr

196

202

W Camano Dr

197

Livingston Bay

BARNUM PT.

Triangle Cove

20E

Monticello Dr

W Camano Dr

195

16E

Bay

LOWELL PT.

EAST POINT

182

Baby Island Rd

Brainers Rd

ROCKY PT.

Goss Lake Rd

HOLMES HARBOR

DINES PT.

Honeymoon Bay

State Hwy 525

Camano Island

160

199

161

ONAMAC PT.

CAMA BEACH SP

PRATTS BLUFF

CAMANO ISLAND SP

184

211

Lagoon Pt Rd

State Hwy 525

SARATOGA PASS

185

167

LONG POINT

SNATELLUM PT.

172 LONG POINT

16E

BLOWERS BLUFF

191

State Hwy 525

Kayaksouy Rd

State Hwy 20

248

240

243

Admiralty Bay

PORT CASSIDY

244

STONE PT.

SOUTH WHIDBEY SP

ADMIRALTY INLET

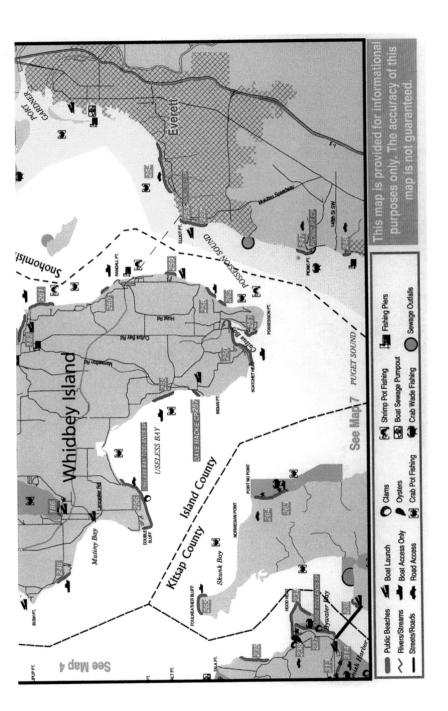

Legend:

Public Beaches
Rivers/Streams
Streets/Roads

Boat Launch
Boat Access Only
Road Access

Clams
Oysters
Crab Pot Fishing

Shrimp Pot Fishing
Boat Sewage Pumpout
Crab Wade Fishing

Fishing Piers
Sewage Outfalls

Whidbey Island

Everett

POSSESSION SOUND

PUGET SOUND

See Map 7

Island County

Kitsap County

Snohomish

PORT GARDNER

Mutiny Bay

Useless Bay

Skunk Bay

See Map 4

USELESS BAY TIDELANDS SP

DAVE MACKIE CP

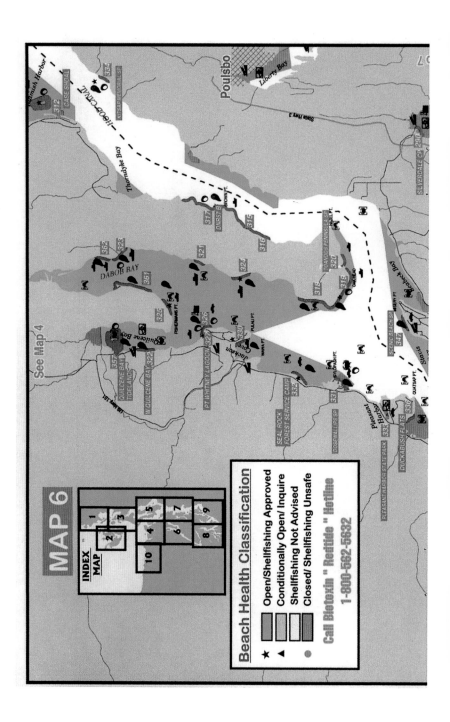

MAP 6

INDEX MAP

Beach Health Classification

★ Open/Shellfishing Approved
◀ Conditionally Open/ Inquire
Shellfishing Not Advised
● Closed/ Shellfishing Unsafe

Call Biotoxin " Redtide " Hotline
1-800-562-5632

See Map 4

Duckabush

Poulsbo

Liberty Bay

State Hwy 3

DABOB BAY

Thorndyke Bay

Quilcene Bay

QUILCENE BAY TIDE LANDS
W QUILCENE BAY
PT WHITNEY LAGOON
SEAL ROCK FOREST SERVICE CAMP
DOSEWALLIPS SP
PLEASANT HARBOR STATE PARK
DUCKABUSH FLATS
Pleasant Harbor

KITSAP MEMORIAL SF
CASE SHOAL
SCENIC BEACH SP

Hammersley Harbor !

92

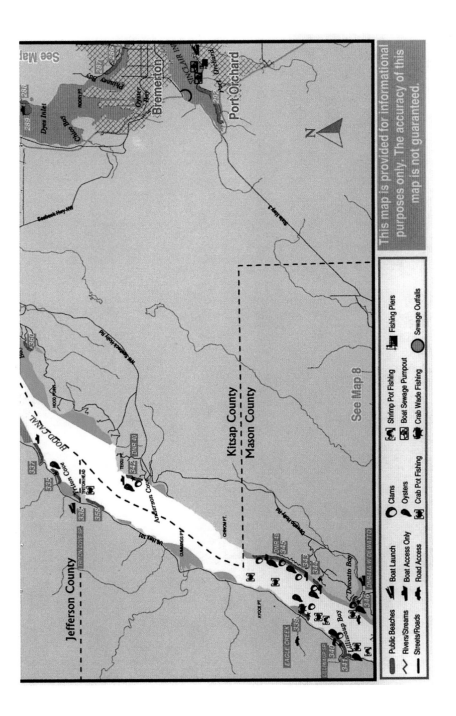

Jefferson County

Kitsap County
Mason County

See Map 8

Bremerton

Port Orchard

HOOD CANAL

Triton Cove

Anderson Cove

Dye's Inlet

Ostrich Bay

Oyster Bay

Phinney Bay

SINCLAIR INLET

Lilliwaup Bay

Dewatto Bay

EAGLE CREEK

TRITON COVE SP

AYOCK PT.

CHINOM PT.

Seabeck Hwy NW

See Map

N

Legend:

Public Beaches

Rivers/Streams

Streets/Roads

Boat Launch

Boat Access Only

Road Access

Clams

Oysters

Crab Pot Fishing

Shrimp Pot Fishing

Boat Sewage Pumpout

Crab Wade Fishing

Fishing Piers

Sewage Outfalls

MAP 7

INDEX MAP

Seattle

See Map 5

Kitsap County
King County

PUGET SOUND

Rolling Bay

Fort Gamble Bay

Poulsbo

Liberty Bay

Hood Canal

Thorndyke Bay

KITSAP MEMORIAL SP

OLD MAN HOUSE SP

FAY BAINBRIDGE SP

Burke Bay

Murden Cove

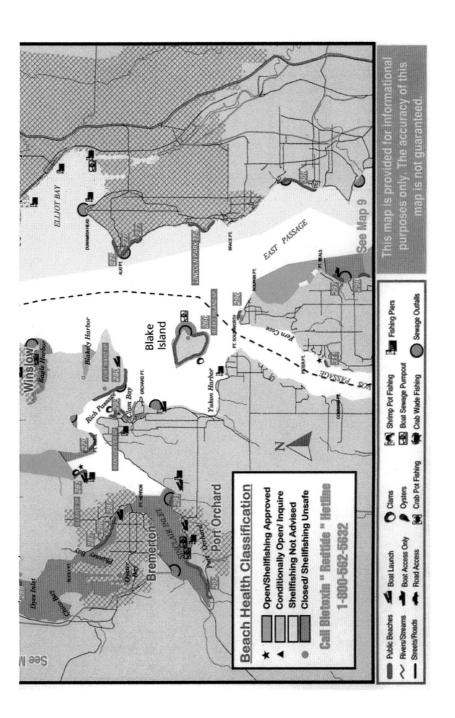

This map is provided for informational purposes only. The accuracy of this map is not guaranteed.

Beach Health Classification

Open/Shellfishing Approved
Conditionally Open/Inquire
Shellfishing Not Advised
Closed/Shellfishing Unsafe

Call Biotoxin "Redtide" Hotline
1-800-562-5632

★ Public Beaches
◄ Rivers/Streams
— Streets/Roads

🡢 Boat Launch
🡡 Boat Access Only
🡠 Road Access

○ Clams
/ Oysters
Crab Pot Fishing

Shrimp Pot Fishing
Boat Sewage Pumpout
Crab Wade Fishing

Fishing Piers
Sewage Outfalls

ELLIOT BAY

DUWAMISH HEAD

ALKI PT.

LINCOLN PARK

BRACE PT.

DOLPHIN PT.

PT. BEALS

EAST PASSAGE

See Map 9

Winslow

Blakely Harbor

Eagle Harbor

Blake Island

BLAKE ISLAND SP.

POINT WHITE

FORT WARD SP.

Rich Passage

ORCHARD PT.

Clam Bay

Yukon Harbor

PT. SOUTHWORTH

Fern Cove

SOUTH PASSAGE

PT. GLOVER

OCEAN PT.

Bremerton

Port Orchard

Port Orchard

PLEASURE

Phinney Bay

Oyster Bay

ROCKY PT.

SINCLAIR INLET

Dyes Inlet

Ostrich Bay

N

See Map

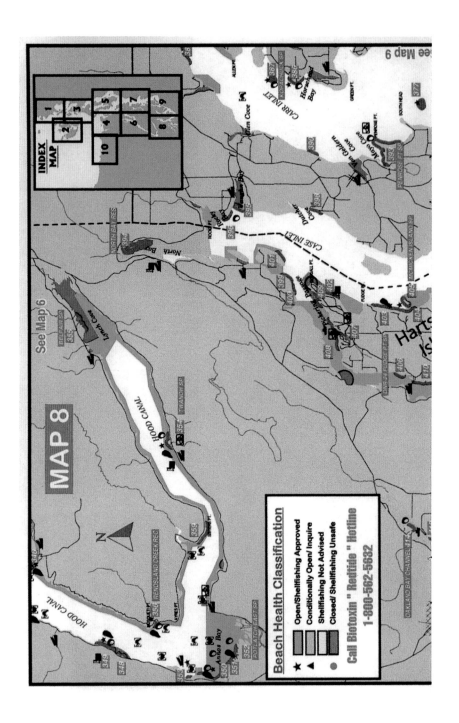

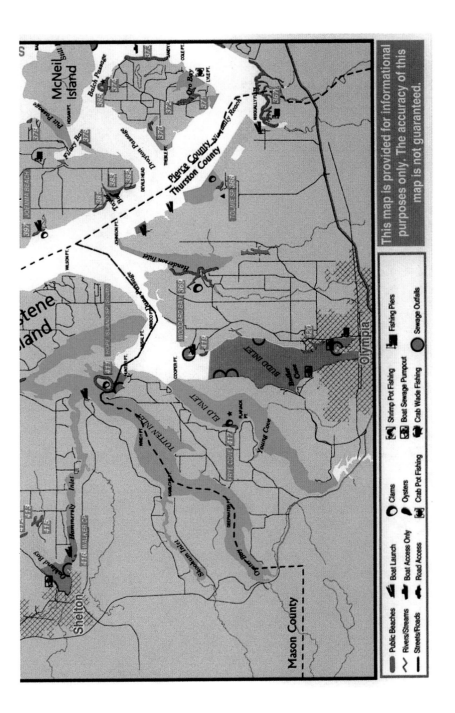

This map is provided for informational purposes only. The accuracy of this map is not guaranteed.

Public Beaches
Rivers/Streams
Streets/Roads

Boat Launch
Boat Access Only
Road Access

Clams
Oysters
Crab Pot Fishing

Shrimp Pot Fishing
Boat Sewage Pumpout
Crab Wade Fishing

Fishing Piers
Sewage Outfalls

97

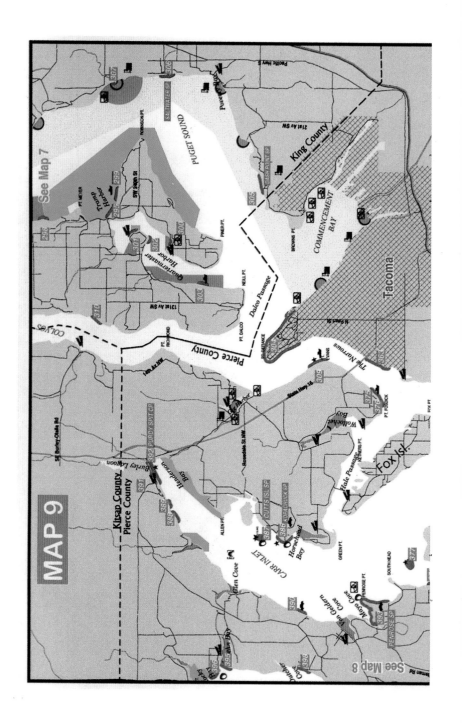

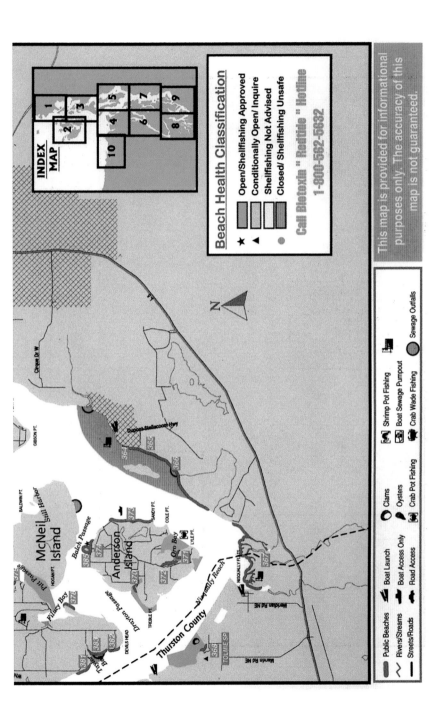

Beach Health Classification

★ Open/Shellfishing Approved
▲ Conditionally Open/ Inquire
● Shellfishing Not Advised
　 Closed/ Shellfishing Unsafe

Call Biotoxin " Redtide " Hotline
1-800-562-5632

This map is provided for informational purposes only. The accuracy of this map is not guaranteed.

Public Beaches
Rivers/Streams
Streets/Roads

Boat Launch
Boat Access Only
Road Access

Clams
Oysters
Crab Pot Fishing

Shrimp Pot Fishing
Boat Sewage Pumpout
Crab Wade Fishing

Sewage Outfalls

INDEX MAP

1 2 3 4 5 6 7 8 9 10

McNeil Island
Still Harbor
Anderson Island
Thurston County
Pitt Passage
Balch Passage
Drayton Passage
Filucy Bay
DEVILS HEAD
Carr Inlet
Nisqually Reach
Oro Bay
TOLMIE SP
Meridian Rd NE
Martin Rd NE
Dupont-Steilacoom Hwy
Chase Dr W

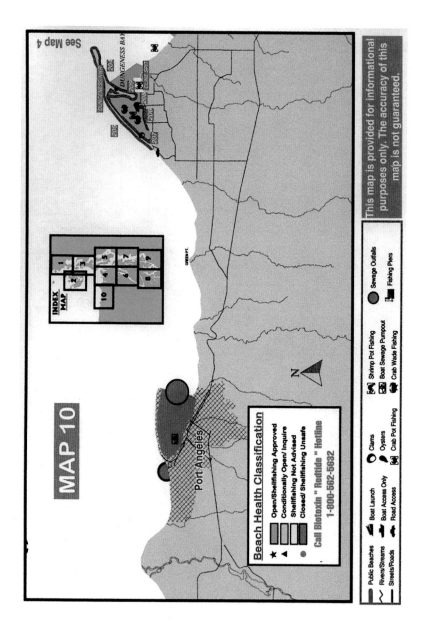

MAP 10

See Map 4

DUNGENESS BAY

DUNGENESS SPIT

20E

20E

20D

20D

20C

20B

20A

GREEN PT.

Port Angeles

INDEX MAP

N

Beach Health Classification

★ Open/Shellfishing Approved

▲ Conditionally Open/ Inquire

   Shellfishing Not Advised

● Closed/ Shellfishing Unsafe

Call Biotoxin " Redtide " Hotline
1-800-562-5632

— Public Beaches
~ Rivers/Streams
— Streets/Roads

⚓ Boat Launch
⚓ Boat Access Only
⚓ Road Access

◗ Clams
◗ Oysters
▨ Crab Pot Fishing

▨ Shrimp Pot Fishing
▨ Boat Sewage Pumpout
🦀 Crab Wade Fishing

● Sewage Outfalls
▥ Fishing Piers

This map is provided for informational purposes only. The accuracy of this map is not guaranteed.

Beach Index — Numerical

Beach Index — Numerical (cont.)

Beach Index — Numerical (cont.)

Appendix B
Oregon Coast Beaches—Northern Half

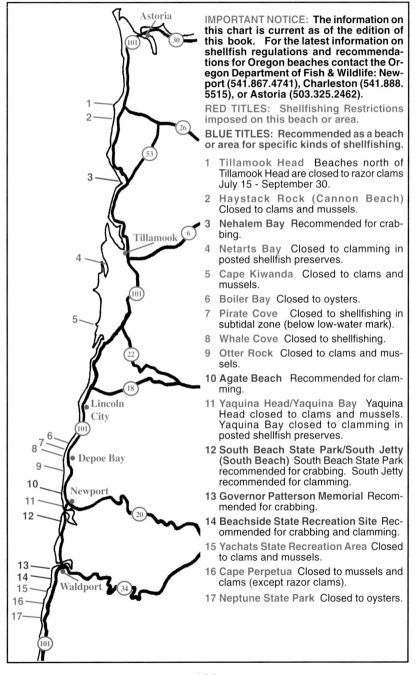

IMPORTANT NOTICE: **The information on this chart is current as of the edition of this book. For the latest information on shellfish regulations and recommendations for Oregon beaches contact the Oregon Department of Fish & Wildlife: Newport (541.867.4741), Charleston (541.888. 5515), or Astoria (503.325.2462).**

RED TITLES: Shellfishing Restrictions imposed on this beach or area.

BLUE TITLES: Recommended as a beach or area for specific kinds of shellfishing.

1 Tillamook Head Beaches north of Tillamook Head are closed to razor clams July 15 - September 30.

2 Haystack Rock (Cannon Beach) Closed to clams and mussels.

3 **Nehalem Bay Recommended for crabbing.**

4 Netarts Bay Closed to clamming in posted shellfish preserves.

5 Cape Kiwanda Closed to clams and mussels.

6 Boiler Bay Closed to oysters.

7 Pirate Cove Closed to shellfishing in subtidal zone (below low-water mark).

8 Whale Cove Closed to shellfishing.

9 Otter Rock Closed to clams and mussels.

10 **Agate Beach Recommended for clamming.**

11 Yaquina Head/Yaquina Bay Yaquina Head closed to clams and mussels. Yaquina Bay closed to clamming in posted shellfish preserves.

12 **South Beach State Park/South Jetty (South Beach)** South Beach State Park recommended for crabbing. South Jetty recommended for clamming.

13 **Governor Patterson Memorial** Recommended for crabbing.

14 **Beachside State Recreation Site** Recommended for crabbing and clamming.

15 Yachats State Recreation Area Closed to clams and mussels.

16 Cape Perpetua Closed to mussels and clams (except razor clams).

17 Neptune State Park Closed to oysters.

Appendix B
Oregon Coast Beaches—Southern Half

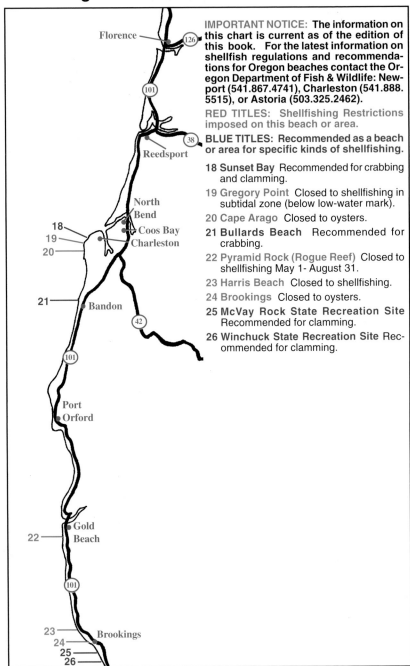

IMPORTANT NOTICE: **The information on this chart is current as of the edition of this book. For the latest information on shellfish regulations and recommendations for Oregon beaches contact the Oregon Department of Fish & Wildlife: Newport (541.867.4741), Charleston (541.888. 5515), or Astoria (503.325.2462).**

RED TITLES: Shellfishing Restrictions imposed on this beach or area.

BLUE TITLES: Recommended as a beach or area for specific kinds of shellfishing.

18 **Sunset Bay** Recommended for crabbing and clamming.

19 Gregory Point Closed to shellfishing in subtidal zone (below low-water mark).

20 Cape Arago Closed to oysters.

21 **Bullards Beach** Recommended for crabbing.

22 Pyramid Rock (Rogue Reef) Closed to shellfishing May 1- August 31.

23 Harris Beach Closed to shellfishing.

24 Brookings Closed to oysters.

25 **McVay Rock State Recreation Site** Recommended for clamming.

26 **Winchuck State Recreation Site** Recommended for clamming.